My Escapes from Japan

Ōsugi Sakae

Translated with an Introduction by
Michael Schauerte

Daikanyama Tokyo

My Escapes from Japan

Translation copyright © 2014 by Michael Schauerte
Afterword copyright © 2014 by Futaba Fukui
Afterword copyright © 2014 by Ōsugi Yutaka
Published 2014 by Doyosha
11-20-305 Sarugaku-cho
Shibuya Tokyo
Japan
All rights reserved

My Escapes from Japan / Ōsugi Sakae
ISBN 978-4-907511-16-6
Printed in the United States

Cover photograph:
The arrest of Ōsugi Sakae on December 12, 1920
at the Kanda Seinen Kaikan
following the Japan Socialist League's inaugural congress.

Image on p.160:
The deportation order issued to Ōsugi in France.

CONTENTS

Translator's Introduction vii
Ōsugi Sakae Chronology (1885–1923) xvii

My Escapes from Japan
Escaping Japan 3
The Toilets of Paris 49
Prison Songs 63
Prison Life until Deportation 71
Assorted Stories from My Trip Overseas 123
A Note to My Comrades 145

Afterword to the 1923 ARS Edition (Kondō Kenji) .. 147
Afterword to the English Edition (Ōsugi Yutaka) 151
Chronology of the "Escapes" (1920–23) 157

Translator's Introduction

Ōsugi Sakae[*] was an anarchist with a sense of humor, some of which he displayed in this book, originally titled *Nippon dasshutsu ki*. Whether its lighthearted tone has survived the transplanting into English, I don't know. The already dry humor may have withered somewhat in the uprooting.

But even in the original Japanese the humor can be overshadowed by the book's sad, unwritten ending: Just over a month before its publication, the military police murdered Ōsugi and his wife Itō Noe and six-year-old nephew Tachibana Munekazu, strangling them to death in Tokyo on September 16, 1923.

---

[*] Japanese names throughout the book are given in the Japanese order, with the surname first.

Not a very funny ending to the story.

And once the postscript is known, this genial book can leave a solemn impression at times. With Ōsugi's death in mind, ordinary incidents leading up to his (forced) return to Japan can seem ominous. Even the title can sound ironic in hindsight, since for Ōsugi there was no escape from the Japanese authorities in the end.

But in November 1922, when the book opens, there is no foreboding of the end. The invitation Ōsugi receives that month to attend an international anarchist congress in Berlin, which he sees as a stroke of good fortune, comes at a point where his future is looking rather bright; certainly much brighter than it had looked a few years earlier.

By this time in his life, Ōsugi has been out of prison for more than a decade (apart from a three-month sentence that began in late 1919). This was quite different from his early years as a radical. He plunged into the socialist movement in 1904, at the age of nineteen, and over the next few years he was in and out of prison several times. By the end of 1910, he had served a total of around three years behind bars.

His time as an inmate was well spent: Ōsugi methodically studied foreign languages ("one crime, one language" became his motto) and read widely to deepen his knowledge of anarchist thought, philosophy, and the natural and social sciences. Looking back on this period, he would write that prison was what formed him, describing his earlier self as ignorant and conceited.[*]

---

[*] Ōsugi Sakae, *Gokuchūki* (Tokyo: Doyosha, 2012) p. 112.

Translator's Introduction

However much he had benefited from the experience, Ōsugi naturally was pleased to be outside the prison walls. Granted, even as a "free" man, he was under constant police surveillance, but this became an ordinary part of his life. And the local uniformed police assigned to the task were a far different breed from the ruthless military police (*kempeitai*) that he had the misfortune to cross paths with later. As Thomas Stanley points out in his biography, "relations between Ōsugi and his [police] shadows seem to have been relaxed, even friendly."[*]

Another cause for optimism by 1922 was that Ōsugi had bounced back from several years of poverty and isolation. His troubles arose from a scandalous "love triangle"—or a really a *square*—that he had entered near the end of 1915. Ōsugi, still married to Hori Yasuko at the time, began simultaneous affairs with Kamichika Ichiko and Itō Noe, two radical women connected to the feminist journal *Seitō* (Bluestockings). By the spring of the next year, newspapers already were reporting sensationally on his infidelities.

Even more shocking to the professed morality of the time was the theory of "free love" espoused by Ōsugi, who for years had been pointing out the ways that class society stunts sexuality and love. He applied elements of this theory, albeit somewhat off-the-cuff, in trying to balance a marriage with two love affairs, proposing that everyone involved abide by three conditions: each person should be economically inde-

---

[*] Thomas Stanley, *Ōsugi Sakae, Anarchist in Taishō Japan: The Creativity of the Ego* (Cambridge: Harvard University Press, 1982) p. 83.

pendent, live separately from one another, and act freely in all matters (including sexual relations). This vision of peaceful coexistence did not stand up very well in practice, however. Not only did his marriage to Hori fall apart, but Ōsugi barely escaped this love experiment alive. On November 8, he was stabbed in the neck by Kamichika, who was angered by his deepening affection for Itō.

He survived the attack, of course, and went on to marry Itō and start a family. But in the aftermath of the scandal many of Ōsugi's old comrades distanced themselves from him, fearing that his "immoral" actions would tar the radical movement. Only by around 1918, when he and Itō began putting out the journal *Bunmei hihyō* (Cultural Review), did his output as a radical writer begin to pick up again.

But these fallow years were well behind Ōsugi by the time of his departure for France. Increasingly he was in demand as a writer and translator. His *Prison Memoirs* (*Gokuchūki*) were published in 1919 and two years later the popular magazine Kaizō began serializing his *Autobiography* (*Jijoden*). So he was no longer sunk in poverty, although still regularly short of funds.

Ōsugi emerged from the low point of his life with his anarchist beliefs firmly intact. His period of poverty and isolation coincided with the outbreak of the Russian Revolution, which spurred many of his old comrades to embrace Bolshevism. Several of Ōsugi's friends from the days of *Heimin shimbun* (Commoners' News), the pioneering socialist newspaper that first drew him into the movement, went on to found the Japanese Communist Party. That Ōsugi did not join these old

Translator's Introduction

comrades in converting to what must have seemed the "winning team" probably owed something to the way they had shunned him after the 1916 scandal.

Yet Ōsugi was willing at first, like many other anarchists at the time, to give the communists the benefit of the doubt. As he writes in this book, he believed that "anarchists and communists could, and indeed should, work together," although he "still maintained the need to respect the freedom of thought and action of each side."

With his goal of a "united front" in mind, Ōsugi traveled to Shanghai in 1920, as he recounts in the book, to attend the Comintern's Conference of Far-Eastern Socialists. But the frustration from that trip and subsequent encounters with communists, combined with what Ōsugi learned about Soviet Russia from Alexander Berkman and others, convinced him that a united front was hopeless. Another factor was the bitter dispute between the two sides in Japan over trade-union organization, which had come to a head by 1923. Ōsugi decides for all of these reasons that he will only work with his "true, anarchist comrades" in the future. And so he seizes on the invitation to attend the anarchist congress in Berlin.

Even though Ōsugi's anarchism is the motive force of the story, insofar as it leads him to Europe, his narrative can be followed easily enough without knowing much if anything about anarchist history.

First of all, the Berlin anarchist congress turns out to be the MacGuffin in the tale. Originally scheduled for late January 1923, the congress is postponed until April and then August, without any clear plan of even where to hold it. Ōsugi would be dead by the time the congress was finally held on October 8 and 9 outside Paris.*

Ōsugi's had other reasons related to anarchism for leaving Japan in 1922, but they do not figure prominently in the book either. He was eager, for instance, to establish contact in Shanghai with members of the recently formed Anarchist Federation, many of whom shared his interest in Esperanto. During his nearly three-week stay in the city, he did meet with those Chinese anarchists a number of times to discuss the Berlin congress and prospects for revolution in China and Japan. But his account of this part of the trip is cursory.

Another aim of his trip was to learn more about the Ukrainian anarchist Nestor Makhno and his peasant army. Indeed, according to Kondō Kenji, the editor of the book's first edition, researching this topic was Ōsugi's "primary task while in France." This is why his August 1923 article on Makhno was added to the ARS edition of the book.† That article was not included in subsequent editions, however, nor is it included in this translation. So in *My Escapes from Japan* you will not come across a single reference to Nestor Makhno, whom Ōsugi named his son after.

There is little need, then, to be familiar with anarchism to follow the events in this book, which was written to entertain,

---

* Tanaka Hikaru, "Ōsugi Sakae ga shusseki dekinakatta anākisuto kokusai kaigi" (The International Anarchist Congress Ōsugi Sakae Could Not Attend), *Shoki shakaishugi kenkyū*, No. 17 (2004), p. 156.

† The 1923 edition includes Ōsugi's article on Makhno as well as his December 1922 article on Marx and Bakunin.

Translator's Introduction

not convert, the reader. Nor is it entirely necessary to know about the events leading up to his departure for France or the tragedy that befell him just two months after his return.

What may be more helpful in orienting oneself as a reader than the background to the author's "escapes" is the history of the book itself. As Ōsugi Yutaka, the author's nephew, notes in his afterword, the chapters in the book (with the exception of the unfinished fifth chapter) were originally published as separate articles. In 1923, *Kaizō* published "Escaping Japan" and "Prison Life until Deportation" in its July and September issues. And the chapters titled "The Toilets of Paris" and "Prison Songs" were serialized in June and July of that year in the newspaper *Tokyo nichinichi shimbun*.

This publication history accounts, in large part, for the overlapping between the chapters, as well as the differences in the exactitude of the author's descriptions. Because Ōsugi was addressing different readers, and wrote the articles at different times, he repeats some of the same anecdotes but leaves out or adds certain details. Descriptions of incidents in Paris overlap between the first two chapters, for example, but the second chapter says nothing about Ōsugi meeting anarchists there.

The final chapter, "Assorted Stories of My Trips Overseas," which Ōsugi did not live to complete, was written specifically for inclusion in the book. But chronologically it fits more neatly within the first chapter since it mainly covers things that happened during the voyage from Shanghai to Marseille. In any case, it may help to keep this patchwork nature of the book in mind while reading it.

My Escapes from Japan

One other thing to contend with is the mark left by the censorship of the time. As in the original text, "×" marks the spot of the censored words or passages, each indicating a deleted Japanese character. I have left in these marks (called *fuseji*) to add some flavor of the original text, but information is provided in brackets, whenever possible, to explain what was deleted.* This English edition also follows the original text in using initials in place of certain names of Ōsugi's friends and comrades, but with footnotes inserted to identify most of them.

I hope that readers will not be too bothered by some of these textual issues; or even appreciate them as traces of the book's time and place. The chronologies may at least prove useful in clarifying the order of events in the book.

But I trust that *My Escapes from Japan* also will stand on its own as a book that brings us into contact with an engaging personality: an anarchist, internationalist, and revolutionary, to be sure, but also a neat-freak and dandy, proud father, philanderer, organizer, a poet, *flâneur*, linguist, sightseer, prison inmate, and lightweight drinker. It is this contradictory man that we encounter in the book, large enough to contain multitudes—and alive to the possibilities (and humor) of every situation.

---

* The restorations are based primarily on the editions of *Nippon dasshutsu ki* that I consulted for my translation: Gendaishichōsha (1965), Iwanami bunko (1971), and Doyosha (2011).

Translator's Introduction

Acknowledgements

Let me borrow this space to thank a few people who helped bring this book to completion.

Ōsugi Yutaka kindly wrote an afterword to this English edition and also provided the chronologies. Ōwada Shigeru took the time to answer a number of questions on passages in the book and introduced me to his fellow editors of the new Pal Shuppan edition of Ōsugi Sakae's complete works. Tanaka Hikaru, Hiyazaki Masaya, Yamaizumi Susumu, and other members of the editorial committee answered various questions related to the translation, and I also benefited from reading their writings on Ōsugi. Finally, I would like to thank Toyota Tsuyoshi of Doyosha for his enthusiastic support of this project and his tremendous patience along the way. Without him, this translation would never have seen the light of day.

No one thanked here is responsible, however, for whatever errors and infelicities are lurking in this English edition: I will have to lay claim to it all as the translator and editor.

Ōsugi Sakae Chronology

(1885–1923)[*]

1885　　Born January 17 in Marugame, Kagawa Prefecture; eldest son of Ōsugi Azuma (then a second lieutenant in the army) and his wife, Toyo. Soon after his birth the family moves to Tokyo.

1889　　Father is transferred to Shibata, Niigata Prefecture, where Ōsugi attends elementary and middle school.

1899　　Enters Nagoya Military Cadet School. Expelled three years later after serious injury in a fight with classmates.

1902　　Moves to Tokyo and enrolls in Tōkyō Gakuin; mother dies suddenly in June. Enters Junten Middle School in October. Interest in social issues sparked by student

---

[*] A slightly modified translation of the chronology by Ōsugi Yutaka in the 2011 Doyosha edition of *Nippon dasshutsu ki*.

protests against pollution incident at the Ashio Copper Mine.

1903 Enters Foreign Language College (today's Tokyo University of Foreign Studies).

1904 Attends weekly meetings on socialism run by the publishers of *Heimin shimbun* (Commoners' News). Begins contributing articles to the newspaper and assisting its editors.

1905 Graduates from Foreign Language College with a degree in French language studies.

1906 Joins the Japan Socialist Party. Arrested and imprisoned for participating in a protest against a streetcar fare hike. Marries Hori Yasuko after release from prison. Opens a school for Esperanto instruction and begins publishing *Katei zasshi* (Home Journal). Indicted for violating Japan's Press Ordinance.

1907 Arrested and imprisoned for five months in Sugamo Prison for his article "*Seinen ni uttau*" (An Appeal to Youth).

1908 Sent back to Sugamo Prison following the Rooftop Speech Incident. Arrested soon after his release in connection to the Red Flag Incident; sentenced to two years in Chiba Prison.

1909 Death of his father.

1910 After release from prison joins Baibunsha, a company run by the socialist Sakai Toshihiko. Kōtoku Shūsui and other radicals are sentenced to death for their alleged role in a plot to assassinate the emperor.

1911 Helps retrieve the bodies of the executed radicals. At-

Ōsugi Sakae Chronology (1885–1923)

tends informal gatherings with comrades every month.

1912 Begins publishing the monthly journal *Kindai shisō* (Modern Thought) with Arahata Kanson.

1913 Comes into contact through *Kindai shisō* with writers and literary figures. Begins a study group on syndicalism.

1914 Ends publication of *Kindai shisō*, replacing it with the more radical monthly publication *Heimin shimbun*. After just four issues the new publication is banned by the government.

1915 Organizes regular lectures on socialism and syndicalism. Revives *Kindai shisō* but after the first issue the government bans distribution. Works as a French instructor.

1916 Halts publication of *Kindai shisō*. Separates from Hori Yasuko and begins living with Itō Noe. Attacked by former mistress Kamichika Ichiko on November 8. Publically criticized for the scandal arising from his infidelities.

1917 Ostracized by former comrades as a result of the previous year's scandal. Ōsugi and Itō struggle financially; birth of daughter Mako in September.

1918 Resumes publication activities with the creation of *Bunmei hihyō* (Critique of Civilization). Starts a study circle on labor movement issues. Begins publication of *Rōdō shimbun* (Labor News) with Wada Kyūtarō and others, but government bans distribution. Witnesses the rice riots in Osaka and takes part to a limited extent.

1919 Begins issuing the monthly *Rōdō undō* (The Labor Movement). Actively supports the labor-union move-

My Escapes from Japan

ment, particularly the printers' union, Seishinkai. Jailed for three months in Toyotama Prison for assaulting a policeman.

1920   Visits labor activists in the Osaka area. Involved in establishing the Japan Socialist League. Makes his way secretly to Shanghai to attend the Comintern's Conference of Far-Eastern Socialists.

1921   Begins issuing the second (weekly) edition of *Rōdō undō* as a "united front" with communists. Hospitalized for typhoid fever. Severs ties with communists and begins the third edition of *Rōdō undō*. Supports the printer union's strike and other labor struggles.

1922   Attends Osaka meeting aimed at establishing a trade-union confederation; conflict between anarchists and communists comes to a head at the meeting. Departs Japan to attend a planned international anarchist conference in Berlin; stops off in Shanghai to meet Chinese comrades.

1923   Arrives in France. Arrested at a May Day meeting in Saint Denis outside Paris and detained at La Santé Prison. Deported from France in June; arrives back in Japan the following month. On September 16, military police abduct and murder Ōsugi along with his wife Itō Noe and six-year-old nephew Tachibana Munekazu.

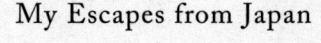

Escaping Japan

I

It was the twentieth of November, last year.* I had crawled into bed just after dinner, a bit tired from work, when M.† brought up a stack of letters for me. Among the usual correspondence from unknown comrades in the provinces was a letter that stood out for its square envelope and Roman script. Taking a closer look, I recognized the sender's name from newspaper articles I had read: it was our French comrade, Colomer.‡

---

* 1922.

† Muraki Genjirō (1890–1925); an anarchist arrested in 1924 for his failed attempt to avenge Ōsugi's murder by assassinating Fukuda Masatarō, the general in charge of martial law after the Great Kanto Earthquake. Died of illness during the preliminary investigation of his case.

‡ André Colomer (1886–1931); editor in the early 1920s of the anarchist

My Escapes from Japan

I held the envelope up to the light, wondering what might be inside. It seemed to contain a single sheet of paper folded into quarters. I took care, as has long been my habit, to examine whether the envelope had been opened somewhere along the way but could find no trace of tampering. Several postal labels were attached, but only because the letter had been mailed to my former residence in Kamakura, then forwarded to a subsequent address in Zushi before finally being sent on to my current lodgings in Tokyo.

Still rather amazed that the envelope had arrived intact after such a meandering journey, I opened it to find a typed letter, just ten lines long. When I read the letter my heart took flight. Colomer had written to invite me to an international congress of anarchists that he was organizing, to be held in Berlin from late January to early February. It was the first I'd heard of the congress, but I decided then and there to attend, for it seemed an ideal opportunity.

I reached over to my small bedside table to grab a copy of the English anarchist paper *Freedom*, still in the envelope in which it had arrived that afternoon. As I had expected, the issue contained an article on the upcoming congress.

*

The article mentioned, just as Colomer had noted in his invitation, that a mid-September gathering in Switzerland had

---

newspaper *le Libertaire* and the journal *la Revue anarchiste*. Joined the French Communist Party in 1927 and died in Moscow.

commemorated the fiftieth anniversary of the 1872 Saint-Imier congress, the first anarchist international. Around a hundred comrades participated in the gathering—from France, Germany, Italy, Switzerland, Russia, as well as China. They included an original participant of the Saint-Imier congress, the Italian anarchist Errico Malatesta, who managed to sneak out of Rome and cross the border into Switzerland, where he risked arrest on sight, having been deported by the Swiss authorities the previous year.

The commemorative meeting served as a sort of international congress where important questions could be raised, such as the role of an anarchist organization and the relation between anarchism and syndicalism. The discussions there culminated with a motion made by the French representative Colomer and others to immediately convene an international congress that would set about organizing a new anarchist league.

The idea of forming an international anarchist league was not new. Fifteen years or so earlier such an organization had been established, at a 1907 congress in Amsterdam. Japan's representative to the league, Kōtoku Shūsui,* submitted a report to it every month detailing our activities. But anarchists at the time tended to look down on any national or interna-

---

* Kōtoku Shūsui (1871–1911); the penname of Kōtoku Denjirō, an early Japanese socialist who veered toward anarchism and "direct action" after spending a year in the United States (1905–6). Arrested in 1910 for his alleged connection to a plot to assassinate the emperor and executed the following year.

tional organization, preferring a movement made up of individuals or small groups. Even when the new league tried to hold a congress, countries did not allow it to convene on their soil, and comrades who hoped to attend were stymied by government repression or a lack of money. Under such conditions the league withered away in a few years.

That 1907 Amsterdam congress was in fact the most recent international meeting to be held successfully. In 1920 another congress was convened in Berlin, but few veteran anarchists attended and the results were meager.

But now time was pressing down on us. The lessons of the Russian Revolution had stirred anarchists everywhere; complacency was no longer acceptable.

*

I was still reading the article in *Freedom* when K.[*] returned from work.

"Look at this letter that's arrived!" I called out to him, and then briefly explained the upcoming congress.

"You can't miss that chance," K. said eagerly.

"Exactly. I just need to come up with the money for the trip."

---

[*] Kondō Kenji (1895–1969); an anarchist who worked closely with Ōsugi on the newspaper *Rōdō undō* (The Labor Movement). In 1922, he was working as an editor for the publishing company ARS (from the Latin for "art"). Later appointed secretary-general of the Japan Anarchist League, established in 1946.

Escaping Japan

"How much do you think you'll need?"

"Hard to say, really. A thousand yen would at least get me there with enough left over to stay a few months."

"As long as you get hold of that much, things should work out. You can figure out the rest later."

"That's what I thought. I'll try rounding up some money tomorrow, and then work out the other details."

"What will you use for a passport?" he asked.

"It's under control. I came up with a way around that problem years ago.* But I'll need to set my plan in motion right away to make it to the congress in time."

K. headed back downstairs, seemingly relieved to hear that the situation was well in hand.

My own mind was not set at ease so readily, however. My prospects for borrowing money were, frankly, dismal. Publishers inclined to lend me money already had, to the point where I could hardly ask for more. And I had submitted few if any of the articles promised them. Even if I could still borrow money from them (and that was something I would *have* to do), it would go toward covering the most pressing needs of the company† and my family while I was away. I did have two or three fairly well-off friends who had lent me some money on occasion, but it seemed unlikely that they could extend me the rather large sum I needed this time. And the

---

* Ōsugi had his associate from anarchist and Esperantist circles, Yamaga Taiji (1892–1970), travel to Shanghai, where he used his contacts to secure a fake Chinese passport.

† Rōdōundōsha, publishers of the newspaper *Rōdō undō*.

business slump of the time only made matters worse.

Lying in bed, I mulled over the situation from every angle without arriving at a clear solution. I would just have to head out early the next morning to see what might be found. Thus resolved, I picked up the scholarly tome on the poet Takarai Kikaku* that I had been duly administering to myself for the past week like a sleeping tablet to dull my mind at night.

The next morning, after shaking off the policemen tailing me, I walked around the city on my quest. Things did not work out as well as I had hoped, however. By evening I was on the verge of giving up and heading home when suddenly I recalled a friend† who might come to my aid. I quickly telephoned this friend—my last, slim hope—and to my surprise he gladly agreed to help me.

*

Now that the needed funds were in hand, my decision to attend the congress was final. The next day I asked M. to tell my wife to return from her hometown in Kyūshū, where she had been staying with two of our daughters. They got back to Tokyo around the time W.‡ arrived from our branch in Kansai.

---

* Takarai Kikaku (1661–1707); a haiku poet and follower of Matsuo Bashō.
† Arishima Takeo (1878–1923); a novelist and founding member of the Shirakaba literary group.
‡ Wada Kyūtarō (1893–1928); a close comrade of Ōsugi. Arrested in 1924 for failed attempt to assassinate General Fukuda Masatarō. Committed

Escaping Japan

No preparations were necessary for my trip. All that I required was a small suitcase. But before leaving I had to finish an article promised to a magazine for its New Year's issue and also complete a book that was to be published around the same time. As I frittered away the days on those tasks, the year was drawing to a close, and my borrowed funds dwindled in half. Finally, on December 11, after getting hold of more money to make up the difference, I slipped out of my house to begin my journey.

II

Sneaking out of my house is something at which I've become quite adept. At times it matters little if the police quickly realize I'm gone, but in other cases prompt detection can make life difficult. Escape in the former case is simple enough, but a bit tricky otherwise.

Two years ago[*] a Russian named Kozlov[†]—who was deported from Japan last summer—snuck out of his home in Hayama to stay at my place in nearby Kamakura, before then fleeing to Kobe. For three days after he left Kamakura, I carried on speaking English in a loud voice inside my house, as

---

    suicide in prison in 1928.

[*] 1921.

[†] Ivan Kozlov; apparently a former IWW member of Russian nationality, born in the United States. Traveled to Japan in 1917 with his wife Clara and spent six years in the country until his deportation in 1922.

if conversing with him. Getting away with a ruse like that for a couple days is one thing, but it's much harder when the deception has to last a whole week or longer.

The year prior to that, I had to slip out of my house in October to make my way to Shanghai. It was important for no one to know about the trip until after I arrived in China, so I departed late at night and arranged for it to seem that I was sick in bed the following day. My house was not very large so any onlooker could easily track my comings and goings. Soon after I snuck out, my police shadows grew rather suspicious. They cornered my daughter Mako, not yet four years old, to figure out where I was. Later, one of the policemen told me what had happened.

"Little Mako was more than we could handle," he recalled. "I asked her: 'Is Daddy home?' And she just gave me a vague, *Hmm*. It seemed odd, so I asked: 'Is Daddy out somewhere?' But again she only answered with a mumble. Still thinking the situation was strange, I tried again: 'So, Daddy is *home*?' But her only reply was another *Hmm*. Finally I said: 'Tell me Mako-chan, is Daddy *home* or *not* at home?' But she just nodded, gave me *Hmm-mmm* and ran off. Over the next ten days I never got a single answer out of your little girl."

This time around, for my latest escape, I was living in the Komagome district of Tokyo, in yet another small house that the police could easily keep an eye on. The agents tailing me were holed up across from the house, in a small shed built on a vacant plot within the grounds of a Shinto shrine. They could tell whether I was at home just by listening to the voices echoing from the house.

Escaping Japan

Mako had turned six by now, which made her that much smarter than two years before. My wife thought it unfair to deceive her about my trip and insisted that we explain the situation so she wouldn't be taken in by the smooth-talking police detectives. But the fact that Mako was smarter hardly set my mind at ease. On the morning of my departure, to avoid any trouble, I had M. take Mako over to the house of our comrade L.,[*] where she could play with another girl just a year or two younger than her.

"This time you can stay over as long as you like," I told Mako, stroking her hair. "How many nights would you like to spend there? Two? *Three?*"

The last time Mako had slept at the girl's house, I picked her up after two days, and she seemed disappointed to see me so soon. So my suggestion of two or three nights did not seem to strike her fancy; she only smiled, without saying a word.

"Well then, how about four or five nights?" I asked.

She smiled and shook her head.

"*More.*"

"How long do you want to stay?" I asked with feigned surprise.

Mako held out the outstretched fingers of one hand on which she placed three more fingers from the other hand.

"Eight days."

"You want to stay *that* long? I said, picking her up to plant a kiss on her cheek. "If you get tired of it over there you can always come home earlier, you know."

---

[*] Identity of L. is unknown.

My Escapes from Japan

When I put her back down she ran off with M., almost dancing away.

She was daddy's little girl—so much so that I'd let her stay with me at the second-floor office in Tokyo rather than going to my wife's hometown in Kyūshū with her younger sisters for a planned six-month stay. Thinking about Mako now I sometimes wonder, no matter how foolish the idea might have been, why I hadn't just taken her along with me to Europe.

Once the situation with Mako had been tidied up, my next task before departing was to decide on some ruse to account for my being out of sight. I resorted, in the end, to my earlier tactic of feigning illness, and had a block of ice delivered to the house several mornings in a row to make my "fever" seem that much more believable.

"That should put them on the wrong track," laughed M., who had come up with the idea, being quite shrewd when faced with such dilemmas.

*

For my departure, K. met me near my house and we sped off in an automobile toward the center of Tokyo. There, near the train station, I purchased a small suitcase and some other items before we hurried off again to catch the train, which was about to depart.

On the platform I looked around but saw no sign of W., who was to meet me and hand over a bundle containing my travel items. Just as I was heading toward the waiting room to

Escaping Japan

have a look inside, I saw a man coming out. From his way of walking I could tell it was W., but he looked different. Instead of his usual old-fashioned velvet suit, which, as I often joked, made him look like a construction hand, he was dressed in a long black cloak that someone must have lent him. As he clanked toward me in his wooden sandals, the brim of his black felt fedora bent upward, he looked every inch the juvenile delinquent.

He handed me the bundle and I jumped on the train. As it left the station, I saw W. on the platform, his hand raised to bid me farewell. I signaled back the same; my final goodbye to the comrades in Japan.

On my previous trip to Shanghai, the comrade who had seen me off was R.,[*] who happened to pay me a visit in Kamakura on the day of my departure. I said nothing to him about where I was going, only that I had to stay out of sight for a while and needed his help.

The two of us walked to the Ōfuna train station, a few kilometers from my home, with R. carrying my suitcase. It was late at night, but some people were still wandering about. The moment we set out I had a premonition that the police had spotted us. As we walked along the road, every car shining its headlights on our backs seemed to be in pursuit, adding to the tension. In Kitakamakura, somewhere between the Kenchō-ji and Engaku-ji temples, an automobile with its

---

[*] Kuwabara Rentarō (1885–1960); member of the printers' union, Seishinkai. Visited Ōsugi on this day to ask him to write a short report on the union's failed newspaper strike of the previous year.

headlights off passed us from behind. A moment later, when the same car—or so it seemed—turned back in our direction, I was almost certain we were on the verge of arrest.

But nothing happened; the car just drove past us. This gave me a strong urge to tell R. where I was headed. Several times I was about to reveal my plans to him, but each time stopped short. It wasn't that R. seemed untrustworthy, only that he hadn't been in our ranks for long and had no direct connection with any comrade strictly within our orbit.

We arrived at the station in Ōfuna, where I boarded the outbound train and R. took the inbound train for Tokyo. Later I heard from K. that R. did not tell anyone about my departure, nor had he asked K. or anyone else where I was headed. Even today, I say a silent word of thanks to R. whenever I see him.

Once W. was no longer visible on the platform, I hiked up the collar of my jacket to shield my face from the train attendant and entered the carriage to climb into the sleeping compartment. I had yet to rid myself of my most distinguishing feature, my moustache. But after a short nap I went to the bathroom and neatly shaved it off. Then I transferred the bundle W. had given me to a suitcase. I had not brought much with me for the trip apart from a few manuscripts that I hoped to work on.

Not long before setting out on my journey I learned from a newspaper article that Japan's "mobile police force"* was to

---

* The Ministry of Home Affairs established a "mobile police force" (*idō keisatsu*) in December 1921 to monitor the movements of left-wing rad-

Escaping Japan

be expanded on December 15 in recognition of its excellent track record. It was unpleasant to imagine that my own arrest might add to this unit's accomplishments. Despite this apprehension, I managed to reach Kobe the morning after my departure without encountering any obvious police agents.

Kobe was hostile territory for me. Around the time Kozlov fled there, police headquarters distributed my photograph to special agents and those in charge of foreign affairs, making it likely that one of the city's many police spies would spot me this time around. This made it risky to board a ship in Kobe, but it was at least less perilous than departing from Yokohama, where you could hardly find a policeman unable to recognize my face since so many had tailed me at one time or another during my many years of living in nearby Kamakura and Zushi.

At the Kobe station only a few people were standing around when I passed through the ticket gate. But one man appeared to be looking at me in a peculiar way. As I walked past he seemed to dash off toward the gate attendant. I exited the station swiftly and jumped into a taxi, instructing the driver to take me to some random destination; and from there I changed cabs to make my way to a hotel.

I purchased a ticket for a ship scheduled to leave the following day, but the departure was delayed until the day after. This left me little choice but to hole up in my hotel room for the two days, using the time to revise a book[*] I was co-

---

icals.

[*] Jean-Henri Fabre's *Souvenirs entomologiques*.

translating. The only time I left the hotel, to take a stroll after lunch, I came across three employees of Kaizōsha.* They were traveling around by automobile to pass out leaflets for a lecture that evening by Albert Einstein. After noticing them, I moved a bit closer to their car, wanting to know if they had spotted me or not. But they paid no attention, even when I was standing nearly in front of them. It didn't surprise me, really. I recalled how once, at a send-off party for me before a prison sentence, I arrived at a restaurant with a short, convict-length haircut and my friends could not recognize me for quite some time, even after I moved from a corner table to one right next to them.

After boarding the ship in Kobe, I noticed that four or five plainclothes policemen were also on board. They were wandering about, and later I saw them loitering in the smoking room near my second-class cabin. It was an unsettling sight, but I relished the chance to toy with them a bit. Instead of staying cooped up in my cabin, I freely moved around the smoking room and deck. Once I even entered the smoking room when only the plainclothesmen were inside and enjoyed a smoke while studying their profiles.

Our ship passed through Moji in the north of Kyūshū before arriving in Nagasaki, where two more plainclothes cops boarded along with four or five uniformed officers. The police for some reason began to question each Japanese passenger. It was an English ship, so there were only four other Japanese traveling in second class with me. I soon was summoned for

---

* The company that published Ōsugi's autobiography in 1923.

Escaping Japan

questioning, but it was over almost as soon as it began. I saw the police had gotten hold of a Filipino student and were peppering him with questions.

At the customs exit in Shanghai, I saw two more men who looked like plainclothesmen—probably part of the squad of four or five agents that the National Police Agency was said to have dispatched to the city.

Once through customs, I quickly hailed a carriage outside. After it had driven on for a while I glanced over my shoulder a few times, but could not see anyone following me.

III

The most perilous moment of my trip, I had imagined, would be disembarking in Shanghai. It seemed the likeliest place for me to be arrested, and I had worked out some escape routes in the hope of avoiding that fate. So it was something of an anticlimax to find myself in a carriage tranquilly clip-clopping away from the dock.

"Take me to the French Concession," was my simple instruction to the driver.

We passed along Da Ma Lu—the Ginza Avenue of Shanghai—before turning off near the entertainment district on Xinshijie and heading toward Dashijie. It was the same route I had taken when in Shanghai the year before last,* and I hope the reader won't mind if I recount a few things about that trip.

---

* 1920.

My Escapes from Japan

*

In late August of that year a young man, whom I shall call M.,* suddenly showed up at my house in Kamakura. He was one of the leaders of the provisional Korean government and had come with regard to a plan to hold the ×××××××, ××, ××××××××××× [CONFERENCE OF FAR-EASTERN SOCIALISTS]† in Shanghai in the near future. This plan now only awaited the participation of a delegate from Japan; a role M. hoped that I might play.

In the past we had worked together to create the ××××××××, ×××××, ××, ××××, ××, ×××××××× [ASIAN FRIENDSHIP SOCIETY], but in the wake of the Red Flag Incident‡ most of the Japanese comrades were thrown in jail, and foreign comrades were placed under tight police surveillance, forcing them to leave Japan. Two years later the High Treason Incident§ oc-

---

* Yi Ch'un-suk; vice-minister of military affairs for the Shanghai-based Korean provisional government, formed in 1919.

† As noted in the introduction, censored passages are indicated using "×" marks, each corresponding to a deleted Japanese character. Bracketed information is provided when the censored text can be reasonably surmised.

‡ At a political rally in Tokyo on June 22, 1908, Ōsugi and several others were arrested and imprisoned for hoisting red flags and displaying revolutionary slogans.

§ A 1910 plot to assassinate the emperor. Twelve radicals, including Kōtoku Shūsui, were executed in January 1911 for their alleged connec-

curred, which severed our contact with overseas comrades for a long time thereafter and also stymied our movement in Japan.

But now, with the proposal for a xxxxxxx [FAR-EAST COMMUNIST LEAGUE] conveyed by the Korean comrade, these contacts were being revived on the narrower basis of adherence to socialism. It struck me as a welcome development, so I immediately took M. up on his offer.

Another reason for my willing response, and perhaps the main reason, was that Sakai* and Yamakawa† had so adamantly refused the same proposal from M.

The Shanghai comrades who had sent M. to Japan as their secret emissary initially wanted xxxxxxxxxxxxxxxxxxxxxxxx [TO MAKE THE JAPAN SOCIALIST LEAGUE THE BRANCH OF THE COMINTERN IN JAPAN]. M. first intended to collaborate with Sakai and met him secretly. But the Japan Socialist League,‡ still under preparation and containing all sorts of political tendencies, was in no position to join forces with the

---

tion to it. Ōsugi only escaped arrest because he already was in prison at the time.

* Sakai Toshihiko (1871–1933); a socialist who in 1903 helped establish the radical newspaper *Heimin shimbun* (Commoners' News) with Kōtoku Shūsui. Later joined the Japanese Communist Party.

† Yamakawa Hitoshi (1880–1958); a contributor to *Heimin shimbun*. One of the founders of the Japanese Communist Party. Later left the JCP to form the dissident Labor-Farmer Faction (*Rōnō ha*).

‡ The Japan Socialist League was established on December 10, 1920; the government ordered it to disband in May 1921.

conference or even bring up the matter at the meeting of its founding committee. The problem, first of all, was that this issue required the utmost secrecy. And second, having the leaders of xxxxxxxxxxxxxxxxxxxxxxxxx participate would bring to light many differences of opinion and be fraught with considerable danger.

Recognizing these difficulties, M. had asked Sakai and Yamakawa to simply participate in the conference as individuals. Both refused, however, for rather feeble reasons. M. then asked if they could at least recommend someone else to attend, mentioning my name as a candidate, apparently. But that request also was turned down. Having no other recourse, M. finally requested that they at least sign some document endorsing the aims of the conference that he could take back to Shanghai. That appeal, too, was rejected.

With little hope left by the time he arrived at my doorstep, M. delivered the same proposal to me. It was easy to see why Sakai and Yamakawa had not known if M. was trustworthy; I wasn't sure myself. There was no way to verify his credentials or letters of recommendation since we were out of contact with comrades overseas. Still, I thought that talking to him for an hour or two would be enough to know whether he was who he claimed to be. If he did seem legitimate, I was willing to go along with his proposal, at least to some extent. My feeling was shaped by the way Sakai and Yamakawa at the time were leaning more or less—or even heavily—toward communism.

The gut feeling they had against M. arose not just from doubts about him personally, but even more from the danger

Escaping Japan

that seemed to surround his proposal. In the worst case, involvement in ××××××××××××××××××× could bring prosecution for criminal insurrection. That fear was weighing on us all, and it accounts in large measure for Sakai and Yamakawa rejecting the Shanghai comrades' invitation.

M. understood the situation well. Coupled with his anguish at the prospect of failing to accomplish his mission, was his despair over what might be called the ×××××××××××× of Japan. In traveling to Japan, he had risked immediate arrest and a prison sentence of who knew how many years. Yet his Japanese "comrades" showed little if any interest in what he was proposing.

This was why, when M. began to tell me about the conference, instead of frankly asking me to join, he was timid and spoke haltingly, his eyes downcast like a disreputable relation who had come begging for a handout. I listened silently to his long, rambling explanation and then, much to his apparent astonishment, simply said, "Great, I'll go!"

*

My own plans for visiting Shanghai stretched back some two years before M. paid me that visit. Whenever I was troubled by the difficulties of our movement in Japan, my thoughts naturally drifted to Shanghai and the chance to renew contact with our comrades in China. The opportunity to travel there finally seemed to be hand at that time, and I made it

My Escapes from Japan

known to Yamakawa and Arahata[*] that I would be traveling to Shanghai. Sakai learned about my plans, in turn, from Yamakawa, but never responded to me about the matter since we had been estranged for some time. Yamakawa and Arahata, for their part, did nothing more than coolly listen to what I had to say, for our relations, too, had chilled considerably. Ultimately, though that first plan to visit Shanghai fell apart, and I had to return to Tokyo before ever setting foot outside Japan.

*

One aim in establishing the Japan Socialist League, along with its general objectives, had been to thaw the relations between formerly close comrades that had chilled over the past decade. The effort was doomed to fail, however. Too many personal differences had emerged between us and our principles and outlooks were diverging steadily. This is why Sakai and Yamakawa did not tell me about the invitation they received from M.; nor did I mention to them my own invitation, fearing they would snub me as they had him. In any event, I thought that I could always tell them about the Shanghai conference after my return if it went well.

---

[*] Arahata Kanson (1887–1981); a socialist who co-founded the journal *Kindai shisō* (Modern Thought) with Ōsugi in 1912. Helped establish the first Japanese Communist Party in 1922, but left it later to join the Labor-Farmer Faction (*Rōnō ha*).

Escaping Japan

*

October arrived, the time of my departure, and I managed to sneak out of my house as already described.

I had sent word by telegraph that I would be arriving in Shanghai and expected someone to be there to greet me. But I disembarked to find no one waiting at the dock. For a while, not knowing what else to do, I paced back and forth in front of the customs house, and then decided to get into one of the horse-drawn carriages that cabbies were incessantly hawking.

I told the driver the address I had memorized in Chinese. On the way there we passed through an array of city districts; some looked wholly European to me; some housing the local Chinese, judging from the banter I overheard; and others simply overflowing with inhabitants.

There were two residences that I had been told to visit, both on the same block. Let's call them apartment "No. 10" and "No. 15." Upon arriving, I first went to No. 10, where M. was supposed to be staying. But the man who opened the door said no one of that name was there. Next I went to No. 15, where I expected to find ×××, but again was told that I had the wrong address. This sent me back to No. 10, where I got the same answer as before. And then it was back to No. 15. Each time I knocked, the tone of the man answering the door was a bit rougher than before. The only thing clear to me was that the men were Korean, as I detected from their accents in Chinese when they were engaged with the coachman in what seemed to be an argument. Finally, I decided to return to No.

10 and plant myself there, no matter what I was told.

At that apartment I was allowed to set foot inside for the first time. I wrote down my name and that of M. and handed it to one of the handful of Koreans surrounding me. One of them went upstairs, and a short while later came back down with another Korean whose face was familiar to me from the ship. It was a man who, during the voyage, had described himself as Japanese and given me the impression of being someone who was to be treated with considerable caution.

"Hey, it's you! I recognize you from the ship," I said brashly in Japanese.

He had spoken in the same forthright way in his conversations on deck with other Japanese. I had made a point of avoiding any conversation with him then, but now that I found myself in this apartment, and my initial hunch about the man turned out to be correct, there was no reason to hold back.

Yet, quite unlike his sociable manner aboard the ship, he ignored my chatter. Paying no attention to what I was saying, he launched into a sort of courtroom interrogation before I had even sat down:

"How is it that you know M.?"

Here we go, I thought. Between puffs on my cigarette I answered his questions frankly, resting an elbow on the table to prop up my cheek. During this grilling I had the impression that M.—who probably had not received my telegram—was peering out at me.

The man kept up the interrogation, the questions coming one after another. At some point, though, the front door opened and in came M., who hurried over to shake my hand. After saying a word to the others, who were now gawking at me, he led the way up to the second floor.

IV

"I must say, you're the first Japanese to ever set foot in here. Only L. and I knew that you were planning to come. But we didn't receive a telegram about your exact arrival."

M. began with these excuses, delivered in quite good Japanese, although not as fluent as my recent inquisitor. The sudden arrival of an unknown Japanese man in a Korean neighborhood had caused something of an upheaval, apparently. After I entered No. 10, M. learned from the carriage driver that I had hailed a cab outside the Japanese consulate, which happens to be right in front of the customs house. This fact made the situation seem even more suspicious in the eyes of M. and his comrades, and they were fully prepared to rub me out if their investigation raised graver doubts.

What made matters worse was that the slip of paper I presented at the apartment with what I thought was M.'s pseudonym turned out to be his real name. M. had taught me two of his assumed names, each made up of two Chinese characters. But the name that I had written down, which hardly any of his comrades knew, had a character from each of those names. It's not so unusual, as any criminologist would know, for a person's real name to bear such a close association to his assumed names.

My Escapes from Japan

When M. heard that an unknown Japanese man who knew his real name had arrived, he surely must have thought a policeman had been sent to arrest him. Yet, knowing the police would hardly dispatch a lone agent, he searched high and low for other policemen hiding somewhere. When the search turned up nothing, he finally decided to come out and see for himself who the Japanese stranger was.

"You know, even after I took a close look at your face and clothes, I couldn't recognize you," M. said. He then took yet another look at the face that apparently bore so little resemblance to my own.

M. led me back to No. 15 to meet L.* Half a dozen men had already gathered in L.'s room to wait for me. In the middle of the room was a man older and larger than the others; his twirled moustache and pointed beard made him look less like an Oriental than a high-ranking French officer. I knew at once that the man must be L., also famous in Japan for his role in the ×××× [RIGHTEOUS ARMY MOVEMENT].† I was presented right away to this man, who did turn out to be L.

"It's been a good ten years," he began by way of introduction (or maybe he said "twenty"), "since I've had an opportunity to sit down with a Japanese; or this might even be the first time for me."

---

* Yi Dong-hwi (1873–1935); prime minister of the Shanghai-based Korean Provisional Government. Also maintained close ties with the Comintern and helped establish the Koryo Communist Party in Shanghai.

† Small armed militias that resisted Japan's colonial rule of Korea; particularly active in the periods 1895–6 and 1905–14.

Escaping Japan

M., who was interpreting for us, went on to explain that L. was a military man who, from the time Korea first became a Japanese protectorate, had ×××××××××××××××××××××××× ×× ××××××××××××××××××××××.

*

L. and I talked for about an hour; then M. took me to a hotel* that L. had recommended. It was said to be first-rate; Chinese-owned, but European in style. Bertrand Russell had apparently stayed there on his recent trip to Shanghai. At the hotel, I was shown to the grandiosely named "×××× Room," but found it to be quite shabby and sparsely decorated: it had no carpet or curtains, and was furnished with nothing more than a dirty makeshift desk, a few chairs, and a bed.

One look around the room made me feel reluctant to stay there. And since I also worried that the hotel would be too expensive, I asked M. if he might escort me to a more modest lodging place. He informed me that the hotel had been chosen because sentiment against Japan in the city made it impossible for a Japanese to stay at any of the smaller hotels. I had become aware of that sentiment as we made our way through the city streets to the hotel and M. pointed out to me the wall posters everywhere urging residents to boycott Japanese goods.

Since I had the added concern of not wanting to draw the

---

* Astor House Hotel.

My Escapes from Japan

attention of the Japanese police, I decided to stay at the hotel recommended by L., registering under a Chinese name.

The conference began on the following day. The half dozen or so participants included the Russian T.,* the Chinese C.,† and the Korean R.‡ We met nearly every other day at the house of C., a former Peking University professor who was later jailed and then fled to Shanghai, where he set up the socialist journal *New Youth* and gained a reputation as an authority on communism. As for R., he had been at the center of a noisy controversy when it was learned that his trip to Japan§ had been made under the auspices of Koga Renzō.¶

Before I left Japan for Shanghai, my comrades had predicted that I would end up arguing with the others, and in fact each session of the conference ended in a dispute between T. and me. During these meetings, T. xxxxxxxxxxx

---

* Grigori Voitinsky (1893–1953); Comintern agent for its Far Eastern Bureau. Sent to China in the spring of 1920 to help establish the Chinese Communist Party.
† Chen Duxiu (1879–1942); co-founder of the Chinese Communist Party and its first general secretary, from 1921 to 1927.
‡ Lyuh Woon-hyung (1886–1947); foreign minister for the Korean Provisional Government and also a member of the Shanghai-based Koryo Communist Party.
§ In 1919, Lyuh Woon-hyung traveled to Tokyo, where he delivered a famous speech at the Imperial Hotel on Korea's "right to life."
¶ Koga Renzō (1858–1942); chief of Japan's Colonization Bureau. Was at the center of a scandal that erupted in 1921 surrounding Japanese corruption in Manchuria, including opium trafficking and bribery.

Escaping Japan

×××
×××. And all of the Chinese comrades, along with the Korean comrades, seemed to be in agreement with this. All that was needed was my consent for the conference to be concluded smoothly.

I believed at the time that anarchists and communists could, and indeed *should*, work together, which is precisely why I joined the Japan Socialist League. But I still maintained the need to respect the freedom of thought and action of each side. And, as an anarchist, I was not willing to join the Far-East Communist League or the Third International. So at the conference I could do little more than state my position that ××××××××××××××××××××××××××××××××××.

From the situations described by the comrades at the conference, I gathered that the Korean representatives were not ardent communists. Rather, seeing the futility of their efforts thus far to achieve independence, they were simply ××××××××××××××××××××, whether that meant relying on socialism, communism, or even anarchism. And though the ranks of the Chinese comrades included C., who ideologically was already quite clearly communistic, their emotions were not yet marked by the "iron discipline" of the Communist Party. Moreover, all of the Asian comrades at the conference disliked how the Russian T. was meddling in the smallest details of the movements in their countries.

The Korean and Chinese comrades thus agreed with my proposal for the revolutionary party in each country to be free to carry out its activities as it liked. If that were to be the case, then ××

My Escapes from Japan

xxxxxxxxxxxxxxxxxxxxxxxxxxxxxxxxxxxxxxxxxxxxxxxxx
xxxxxxxxxxxxxxxxxxxxxxxx.

*

After the conference discussions, T. told me that he wanted to talk about something in private, and he led me to the room where he was staying.

What T. wanted to discuss came down to money. He offered to provide our movement in Japan with funds, and wanted to know about our current plans and how much money they might require. I told him that, for the moment, our only plan was the modest one of putting out a weekly newspaper, and that ten thousand yen would cover publication for half a year, after which we could manage on our own.

T. agreed to supply that money right away. But later, when I met with him again a number of times, he began to pester me for details about the content of the newspaper. Neither my personality nor my principles allowed me to tolerate such meddling.

Ultimately, I told T. that I wasn't interested in receiving his funds, just as I had threatened earlier to return to Japan if his intrusive ways continued. I made it plain that my reason for coming to Shanghai was not to raise funds but to establish contact with the comrades in East Asia. Now that contact had been established, I argued, it was best to let the movement in each country advance in its own way. Our movement in Japan had unfolded in that way up to then, following its own path regardless of the source of funding, and that orientation wouldn't change in the future. Money with strings attached held no interest. I conveyed this to T. in our discussions, which were conducted in English through the exchange of written notes.

T. consented and promised just to provide money to fund our movement whenever necessary. In the end, however, I only received two thousand yen from him just prior to my departure, along with the excuse that money was "a bit tight" at the moment.

*

Once I got back to Japan from Shanghai, I explained the details of the conference to Sakai, who relayed the information to Yamakawa. And the three of us decided to meet again. In our discussion I suggested that they should run the newspaper because I had promised to visit Russia in the near future; and that, in any case, the work in Shanghai was better suited to communists. They didn't respond directly, however, and later a comrade told me that they hadn't even considered my proposal seriously.

What emerged eventually was the weekly newspaper *Rōdō undō* (The Labor Movement), established by comrades with whom I had once promised to create a monthly: the anarchists Kondō Kenji and Wada Kyūtarō and several communists, including Kondō Eizō[*] (also known as Ii Kei) and

---

[*] Kondō Eizō (1883–1965); a founding member of the Japanese Communist Party. Drifted away from the JCP to join the Labor-Farmer Party

Takatsu Masamichi.* I had been warned by Sakai that Kondō Eizō would be reluctant to work with an anarchist like me, but Kondō laughed when he heard that, and I joined in his laughter.

From the outset I wanted these comrades to handle the newspaper. My plan was to head off to Russia as soon as the newspaper took shape, but I fell ill before the project began. For quite some time I suffered from the illness and even after my lungs seemed to improve it flared up again. My doctor insisted that I rest. During my convalescence, while comrades were preparing the newspaper, I also contracted typhus.

These health problems severed my contact with the committee in Shanghai. And the money T. had promised to send right away never materialized. Despite this, the comrades in Japan pulled together and Kondō Kenji managed to borrow money for the newspaper, which was published under my name. The newspaper ran until June, but I was still recovering my health after leaving hospital so I didn't contribute many articles.

In April of that year or thereabouts, we sent Kondō Eizō to Shanghai to reestablish contact with the comrades there and bring back the funds that had been promised us. After Kondō left, though, I had a strong suspicion that he and Takatsu—

(*Rōdōnōmin tō*); later converted to "state socialism" (*kokka shakaishugi*).

* Takatsu Masamichi (1893–1974); a leading member of the early Japanese Communist Party. Left the JCP in 1927 to join the Labor-Farmer Party. Helped establish the Japan Proletarian Party (*Nihon musantō*) in 1937.

Escaping Japan

in cahoots with Sakai, Yamakawa, and others—were secretly maneuvering to exclude anarchists from their plans. If so, I preferred to just let the communists take charge of the relations with Shanghai, which was a direction toward which I thought Kondō was already headed. We anarchists, meanwhile, could start up a new project of our own. In the event, Kondō was arrested* on his way back from Shanghai, and that served as the pretext for halting publication of the newspaper.

When Kondō was released from jail, a month or so later, he only met with Yamakawa before moving to Kobe to be reunited with his and wife and child. Yamakawa conveyed Kondō's message to me that T., although not in Shanghai at the time, had relayed two thousand yen through a Korean comrade to pay for my trip to Russia and another two hundred as condolence money for my illness. This story was quite different from the account I had heard (but could not confirm) from my comrades. It really didn't matter, though; I was simply glad to break off relations with the communists.

Perhaps because of the reluctance of T., the committee set up in Shanghai seemed to fade away without carrying out any work after my return to Japan. At any rate, as he confessed to the police, Kondō Eizō received around six thousand yen from a Korean on the committee.

---

* Kondō Eizō returned to Japan from Shanghai on May 30, 1921 with the enormous sum of at least 6,000 yen received from the Comintern. He managed to get himself arrested soon after disembarking in Shimonoseki (Yamaguchi Prefecture) as a result of his drunken escapades after missing the express train to Tokyo.

My Escapes from Japan

*

This excursion into events before my recent trip to Europe stirs up some rather unpleasant memories. An article I later wrote mocking the communists as a "band of swindlers" was alluding in part to those events. It became increasingly clear to me that the "dictatorship of the proletariat," that beautiful (?) label with which the new communist regime has glorified itself, conceals the fact that the putative dictators, the proletariat, have been enslaved.

I finally woke up to the fact that it wasn't possible, either practically or logically, for me to work with the communists. Even more importantly, I realized that the Communist Party, like capitalist political parties, is hostile to anarchists, and in fact our most insidious foe.

I do owe the communist leaders at least one debt of gratitude, though. Thanks to all the secrets they squealed to the police about their own comrades, I've been able to go into more detail here about my trip to Shanghai.

V

Despite all that that had happened in the meantime, I kept in mind my promise to visit Russia. All during my convalescence and while our plans for a new journal went forward, I quietly awaited that opportunity, longing to see for myself the situation in Russia and travel across Europe to witness the chaotic postwar social and labor movements.

Around October of that year,* it suddenly came to my attention that in Russia ××××××××××××××××××× [THE FIRST CONGRESS OF THE TOILERS OF THE FAR EAST] would be held. A Communist Party member visited me with regard to the meeting. Apparently no workers connected with the communists were willing to attend. I agreed to be one of Japan's ten delegates, but feared the congress would end up like the meeting in Shanghai. Later, in my discussions with communists about the upcoming congress, various hassles arose. It became increasingly clear that the trip would be a waste of time, and just a few days before my planned departure I backed out of it

In January we began publishing a monthly edition of *Rōdō undō*. For nearly every issue I channeled my energy toward exposing the anti-proletarian, anti-revolutionary essence of the Soviet government, sharing the news coming to light of the persecution of anarchists and syndicalists there.

The first occasion for anarchists and communists in Japan to publically air their fundamental theoretical differences was in late August, at a general meeting in Osaka to establish a national labor-union confederation. Workers were divided between those two opposing camps, with one side insisting on centralized leadership and the other calling for a free alliance of autonomous unions.

This was an opportunity for the workers' movement to break new ground theoretically and practically, which ac-

---

* 1921.

counts for the incredibly strained atmosphere at the meeting. It was around this time that the letter ×××××××× [FROM COLOMER] arrived. Departing Japan in the midst of such events, even for a short time, was regrettable; it was agonizing to leave behind comrades so busy that they barely had time to eat or sleep. But I decided to let the Japanese movement take care of itself, knowing that everyone would do their best whether I was there or not. Besides, it was a chance to engage in discussions with comrades overseas—our true, *anarchist* comrades. That's why I resolved so quickly to make the voyage to Europe.

*

On my previous trip to Shanghai, I stayed at three or four hotels for around ten days each, as it was too dangerous for me to stay at any one place for too long. Each time, before checking into the next hotel, I came up with a new pseudonym. Remembering whatever name I happened to be using was not easy. I had to commit to memory the characters for each name and the Chinese pronunciation—two separate things that have no association in the mind of a Japanese. I managed to memorize the names, but it was odd for a man supposedly from China to be unable to speak a word of Chinese. My way of getting around that inconvenience was to use English with the bellboys. I was able to appear convincing by speaking only when it was necessary for some transaction.

Using a false name did trip me up, rather remarkably, on

Escaping Japan

one occasion, though. I had made contact with the Korean R.[*] to put me in touch with his friend, a member of the Kuomintang in Shanghai. When R. went to the house of that friend and found out that he was away on a trip, he wrote down the name of the hotel where I was staying so that his friend could find me later. After returning from his trip, the friend immediately went to my hotel. Since he knew that I must be staying under a false name, he asked if there were any Japanese guests. When the receptionist said no, he asked if there were any Japanese-looking Chinese, but again the answer was no. Not knowing what else to do he had a look at the hotel register listing the names and room numbers of the guests.

"That's him! No doubt about it."

One look at the name on the register was enough for him to know it was me. He marched off to the room listed, where he did indeed find me.

"I can't believe anyone would use such a ridiculous name," he said, bent over with laughter.

"What's wrong with it?" I asked in all seriousness, having no idea what was so funny. "A Korean thought up with that name for me."

"I'll tell you what's wrong with it: *Táng* Semin? It's the same surname as Emperor Táng Tàizōng! In Japan, that would be like calling yourself Toyotomi Hideyoshi or Tokugawa Ieyasu. But I have to hand it to you: thanks to that name I had no trouble tracking you down. A real Chinese would never think of registering under such a name."

---

[*] Lyuh Woon-hyung (see footnote on p. 28).

My Escapes from Japan

If this friend had not found me that evening, I wouldn't have seen him for some time. He was leaving Shanghai the next morning to join the advance contingent of Sun Yat-sen in Guangdong.

"Once we have the new government up and running, you must come to visit us in Guangdong," he said. "Chen Jiongming* is just a warlord and not very sophisticated, but he takes a keen interest in social problems. When we get there we'll surely come under pressure from Chinese and foreign capitalists, but we plan to breathe new life into the workers movement."

This friend—now every inch the politician, but once an ardent labor activist—was emphasizing the workers movement out of political necessity for the new government. This was around the time that anarchists were active in creating labor unions under the banner of defending Chen Jiongming. And Guangdong had become the center of China's labor movement. The anarchists were behind a subsequent major demonstration of deckhands and dockworkers in Hong Kong.

Since I hadn't been able to meet any anarchists in Shanghai, I hoped to encounter some in Guangdong. So, as we bid each other farewell, I promised this up-and-coming politician that I would meet him there in the near future.

---

* Chen Jiongming (1878–1933); the governor of Guangdong. At the time of Ōsugi's first trip to Shanghai, Chen was allied to Sun Yat-sen, but their alliance fell apart in 1922.

Escaping Japan

*

On my second trip to Shanghai, I couldn't stay at the same hotels as before—thanks, again, to the communists blabbing to the police. Since the arrest of Kondō Eizō, the Japanese government had become especially vigilant in Shanghai, and I figured that they knew where I had stayed in the past.

The first thing I did in Shanghai was visit the house of a Chinese comrade, B. It was the first time for us to meet, but we had been in fairly regular contact with each other since the summer through the Chinese comrade W., who had secretly made his way to Tokyo. My reason for coming to Shanghai was not only because ××××××××× [AN INTERNATIONAL CONGRESS OF ANARCHISTS IN BERLIN] was being organized, but also the desire to plan ××××××× [A LEAGUE OF ASIAN ANARCHISTS], which was an even more important task as far as we were concerned.

Regrettably, B. was not at home when I arrived. No one there spoke anything but Chinese and I couldn't leave a written message. I was at a loss for what to do. The Chinese and Koreans whom I had known from before had probably all left for Russia by then. I reckoned that my Kuomintang politician friend was back in Shanghai now that Chen Jiongming's rebellion had taken Guangdong, but I didn't know where to find him. I considered my options: I could let B. know somehow that I had arrived, although it seemed rather pointless by now; or I could look for a hotel run by Westerners; or perhaps it was better to just sit tight and wait for B. to come find me.

My Escapes from Japan

Still tired from the typhoon that had buffeted me from Nagasaki to Shanghai, and since it sounded like B. might return soon (and I had no idea what else to do), I sat myself down in a chair in the entranceway of his apartment to wait for a while.

Before long, a young Chinese man came by where I was waiting. I was taken aback to see a familiar face: it was N.,[*] whom I had met often in Tokyo during the previous year. He had called himself an anarchist at the time and was involved with all sorts of anarchist groups and meetings. But I wasn't sure how far he could be trusted. And I hadn't known that he was going to return to China or what he planned to do there. Far from thinking his arrival a welcome sign, I wasn't even sure if I should let him see me, for I made it a point to avoid anyone who was not in contact with other comrades I knew.

He looked in my direction, and I seemed to notice a trace of surprise in his expression. But I relaxed a bit, soon after, when I realized that he didn't recognize me.

He spoke to someone who seemed to be the doorman, and relayed to me in Japanese that B. should be returning soon. Yet it seemed strange that the man continued to have an air of surprise even though he hadn't recognized me. So, to tease him a bit, I said, in a serious tone:

"You must have lived in Japan for quite a while."

"No, I've never been to Japan," was his surprisingly dour response.

It struck me that he must be have been hassled quite a lot

---

[*] Actual names of B., W., and N. are unknown.

by the Japanese police for his part in the anti-Japan boycott. Perhaps he took me for a typical Japanese or even a rather dubious character. But that only made me want to tease him a bit more.

"But your Japanese is really good, you know."

"No, I don't speak it well at all," he said even more grimly as he flipped through a Chinese newspaper on the table.

The situation was getting odder and odder, but I also felt a bit sorry for him. So I took his response as my cue to be quiet, figuring it would only cause trouble to talk too much. He turned his back on me and kept reading his newspaper.

While I was waiting there, B. returned. I discretely slipped him a written message so he would introduce me to N. under a false name.

The next day, when walking around the neighborhood where B. lived, I came across a boarding house run by a Russian where I was able to get a room without paying anything in advance.

I avoided eating meals in the dining hall, taking my meals in my room instead. So the landlady and the other boarders hardly saw my face. Even after a few days no one came to make me sign the guestbook or present a calling card. Thinking the situation a bit perilous, I asked the bellboy if he knew what country I was from. Without a moment's hesitation he said:

"You're an Englishman."

"Why do you think that," I asked, rather surprised by his answer.

"That's what the landlady said."

There wasn't a trace of doubt in the bellboy's comment, delivered in English every bit as bad as the landlady's, and even worse than my own.

They had obviously mistaken me for a man who was half-English, half-Chinese; a misunderstanding that suited me perfectly. That night, when the bellboy brought up my dinner, he said that few if any Asians stayed at the boardinghouse; almost all of the guests were Europeans.

VI

As for what I did in Shanghai during the few days I was there . . . well, I can't reveal anything for the moment. Let me just say that while in the city I learned of the postponement of the Berlin congress, and this gave me ample time to accomplish my objectives.[*]

During my stay in Shanghai I came across various rumors in the newspapers about my whereabouts. Some claimed that I was in Japan at a hot springs resort in the mountains of Shinshū; others that I had traveled by ship from Harbin to Russia or from Hong Kong to Europe; and still others insisted that I had already been arrested somewhere. Similar rumors even appeared in the Chinese-language press in Shang-

---

[*] While in Shanghai (from December 17, 1922 to January 5, 1923), Ōsugi held discussions with members of the newly formed Anarchist Federation and obtained a Chinese passport and letters of introduction to Chinese comrades in Lyon.

Escaping Japan

hai, along with the claim that I was receiving money every month from Russia to fund my propaganda.

*

All I am able to say here is that on a certain date in 1923, I departed Shanghai on a certain ocean liner[*] belonging to a certain country to make my way to attend the congress scheduled to begin on the first of April. What I did over the course of that trip, however, is not something that I'm able to reveal yet.

(And even now that I've returned to Japan, I still can't recount more about my activities in Shanghai. Let me just say that it's not true, as I wrote above, that I learned while there that the Berlin congress had been postponed and read those false rumors in the newspapers. The truth is that I only became aware of all that after arriving in Paris. In a separate article I'll explain what happened during the time in between.)

So, on a *certain* day—I hope the reader will forgive the frequent repetition of this unavoidable word—I arrived in Paris by a certain route, traveling on a certain ship.

From the return address on Colomer's letter, I knew that the office of the publishers of *le Libertaire*, the newspaper of l'Union anarchiste,[†] was on boulevard de Belleville. Judging from my map of Paris, it was a major thoroughfare, much like

---

[*] Ōsugi departed Shanghai on January 5, 1923 aboard the French ship André Lebon and arrived in Marseille on February 13.

[†] A French anarchist organization established in 1920.

the famous avenue de l'Opéra.

I had imagined the office would be on some side street or attic room but when I got there I saw it was in fact right on the main thoroughfare, very much like the Tokyo street heading from Asakusa to Man'nenchō. Boulevard de Belleville was lined with tall apartments, five, six, or even seven stories tall, but all caked in soot. Perhaps because of the automobile traffic, even the goods in the stores were filthy. And on the wide promenade in the middle of the boulevard dirty tents and sheds were set up around which people swarmed, their grimy, savage faces unlike anything I could imagine seeing in Japan. It was a marketplace, although the stalls hardly looked like shops to me. I saw people walking around with large bags containing what seemed to be their morning groceries: giant heads of cabbage, potatoes, and long loaves of bread.

The Libertaire office was on the ground floor. Along with publishing the weekly newspaper *le Libertaire*, the office put out the monthly journal *la Revue anarchiste* and ran a small publishing company, la Librairie sociale.

Stepping inside, I saw over half a dozen men, similar in appearance and demeanor, absorbed in what seemed a noisy discussion. I asked if Colomer was in and was told he was in the back. It was not that far back, actually; a dirty adjoining room, easily visible from the front. There I encountered seven or eight others partaking in another lively debate, and two men—looking much like everyone else—engaged in some sort of work at their desks.

One man, who was standing next to another desk, rapidly sorting a stack of letters, stood out from the others somewhat

Escaping Japan

in appearance and bearing. He was dressed in relatively clean black clothes and wore a necktie. His long hair framed and accentuated a white face, giving him an artistic appearance. *This must be Colomer*, I thought, and headed over to greet him.

"Yes, I'm Colomer," he said, holding out his hand to me.

Once I had introduced myself he welcomed me heartily, firmly holding on to my hand as he thanked me for making such a long journey. Even before I had sat down, he began to ask me about the situation in Japan.

*

"I'd like to find a place nearby to stay," I mentioned at some point.

"I'll show you around," someone standing behind me said. I turned to find a young woman, short even by Japanese standards, with thick lips and skin that was far from white. Only her large round eyes made her seem European. In general appearance, she was no different from the rough-looking types I had seen around the neighborhood.

The woman led me a few blocks away from the office. We stepped into a narrow side street where nearly every building had a "Hôtel" sign hanging out front, all of them filthy-looking dumps.

"Let's go in and have a look," she said, pointing to one place that didn't seem quite as bad as the rest.

The sign read, *le Grand Hôtel*, but stepping inside I could see it was a ramshackle boardinghouse. A room was available and the concierge took me up to the third floor to have a look.

It was a small room, with no carpet or anything else covering the floor. There was barely enough room for a double bed, a large dresser with a mirror, a desk, two chairs, a ceramic water basin, and a sink with a metal washing board. In one corner there was also a gas stove for cooking simple meals. Everything was coated with layer upon layer of dirt and bore an assortment of defects and blemishes. And over it all lingered an unpleasant smell. But at least the room was much brighter than the dark stairwell and hallway I had passed through to get to it, and its window offered a view that stretched quite far off into the distance.

"Nice, isn't it?" my female guide said, wearing a look of pride.

To my eyes it did not look in the least bit nice. In fact, of all the places where I had stayed over the course of my life, I'd never encountered any room quite so bad. But one of my aims in coming to France had been to get a first-hand look at workers' quarters and possibly stay with a working-class family. Curious about what living in such a place would be like, and not having any alternative, I told the concierge:

"It should be fine. I'll take it."*

First I paid a hundred francs to hire the room for a month (around 12.50 yen by the exchange rate of the time), which worked out to be much cheaper per night than the fifty sen that guests pay at most Tokyo boardinghouses. And by just inserting a one-centime coin I could run the gas long enough

---

* According to French police records, Ōsugi stayed at 3 rue Lemon (a tiny side street just off boulevard de Belleville) from February 24 to March 7.

Escaping Japan

to cook about three meals.

After I paid, the concierge asked me to sign the hotel register. As I had done at other hotels, I simply wrote down whatever name came to mind. But she then asked me to show my *carte d'identité*. Not knowing what that was, I asked the woman who had led me to the hotel to explain. She said that every foreigner in France, as well as French citizens, must carry an identification card. Of course I didn't have one. But the woman and I managed to fudge our way through.

"The French are so strict," I mumbled to her as we headed back to the office to gather my things.

"Yes, without your identification papers the police can grab you anytime and charge an immediate fine, or even throw you in prison. And for foreigners the next step is deportation."

Before she had even finished her explanation we saw three uniformed officers patrolling the corner opposite the Libertaire office. They seemed to be keeping a sharp eye on the entrance.

"It looks like the police," I said, sensing something a bit strange.

"Ever since the Berton Incident they've been patrolling around here regularly."

The woman recounted how an anarchist woman named Germaine Berton[*] had recently assassinated a leader of the

---

[*] Germaine Berton (1902–42) assassinated Action française politician Marius Plateau (1886–1923) on January 22, 1923. At her trial, she declared that the act was done to protest the occupation of the Ruhr and avenge the assassination of Jean Jaurès.

royalist party, and that since then meetings had been strictly monitored, apartments searched, publications checked, and activists tailed and arrested without hesitation.

Reminds me of Japan, I thought as I entered the office, figuring I had drawn the attention of the patrolling officers.

April 5, 1923 – Lyon

The Toilets of Paris

I

Soon after arriving in Paris, a woman[*] ushered me to a hotel in the same neighborhood where a group of her friends regularly met.

It seemed to be a true working-class district. Nearly every storefront was either a cheap café or restaurant or a shabby hotel. As I walked along the streets with the woman, reading the signs for the cut-rate hotels, I wondered where she might be leading me. Some of the hotel rooms could be had for a day or just part of the night. Even lower down the scale were the rooms described as *très confortable*, often without a toilet or even lacking electric lights. Not having a toilet I could understand, but no *lights*—in modern-day Paris!

---

[*] This is the same hotel and woman (an Italian anarchist) mentioned at the end of the first chapter.

My Escapes from Japan

When I told the woman how surprised I was by this she said there were many such rooms in Paris, and that even in the city center some homes relied on oil lamps to this day. Wanting to see such places for myself, I asked her to show me one of the *très confortable* rooms.

She and I went up to a third-floor room of "le Grand Hôtel" (or some such name), equipped with lights but no toilet.

"Where's the toilet" I asked the concierge, thinking the sign outside had been a bit misleading.

"Near the second-floor stairway," she answered blandly.

I went there to take a look and saw it wasn't a Western-style, sit-down toilet, but just a tile floor that slanted toward a small hole at the bottom. You had to straddle your legs over the tiles, around where the slope began. It was far dirtier than any toilet I'd ever set eyes on in Japan.

While staying at the hotel I couldn't bring myself to use that toilet. Instead, I urinated in a bucket I kept in the room for that purpose. There was a washstand but no running water. The water had to be brought up each time from below, and the dirty water then dumped back in the bucket. And it wasn't just my room: I could hear the sound of tinkling in buckets in the adjacent rooms. A proper bowel movement was an even trickier proposition. I had to head out from the side street into the main boulevard and use a pay toilet there that I had come across. If I paid the attendant a bit more, fifty centimes instead of twenty, I could get access to a very clean Western-style toilet.

People in Japan shouldn't think that such experiences were solely the result of living in a run-down boardinghouse. I saw rooms all over Paris in the weeks that followed, but none was equipped with a clean, modern toilet. What I encountered instead, in every apartment and hotel, were dirty, smelly toilets. And it was the same in the countryside.

I had expected the baths to be comfortable, like my initial hopes for the toilets, but among the cheap, *très comfortable* hotels I never saw one with a sign outside promising a bath. Very few ordinary homes were equipped with a bath, either. Men and women only bathed once a month, or every two months, so the scarcity of baths was no surprise. There were a handful of pay baths, nearly as rare as pay toilets. I was lucky to find one not too far from my hotel. I soon became a regular customer, splurging every other day or so by paying two-and-a-half francs for a bath. For less than half that price, I could enjoy a very nice meal in the same neighborhood.

II

I don't want to imply that my entire time in Paris was spent living like a down-and-out in a cheap hotel. I also stayed at a hotel frequented by a more bourgeois clientele, although it was not so terribly luxurious either.

My reason for leaving the rundown hotel was that the police were patrolling that district frequented by my friends day and night. It seemed wise to flee the glare of those watchful eyes.

The next hotel room was a step up, with hot or cold water at the turn of a spout as well as a Western-style bath and toilet.

After dropping my drawers to use the facilities for the first time, it was with some trepidation that I pulled the chord, ever so gently and watched the water flow down. But everything was washed away, beautifully.

I mentioned my concern about toilets to a friend later, who told me there was nothing to worry about. "Our French toilet bowls are wide enough for a baby's head to pass through," he said. But he told me how his Gallic attitude to the commode had backfired in Germany when his drawers fell into the toilet bowl and stopped up the pipes, earning him a stern lecture from the proprietress and a bill for cleaning up the mess.

Another object in my hotel room that I found perplexing was a clean porcelain basin in the corner. It was about the size and shape of a squat toilet, with hot and cold water faucets attached to its raised hood. The sides of this gourd-like object were slightly indented near the middle, where it looked like a person could easily crouch down. But the hole at the bottom was too small for it to be used as a toilet. I could see no reason why I should bathe myself in this basin, either, since the room also had a perfectly serviceable bathtub. When I turned the handle to see what would happen, a powerful jet of water surged out. It was the same sound of gushing water that I had heard in the room next door late at night, just after overhearing what seemed to be the voices of a man and a woman.

I slept on a large double bed on which two pillows were always arranged—as had been the case at the cheap place where I stayed earlier.

For my first night in Paris, I dined at a dingy restaurant,

paying three-and-a-half francs for a *prix fixe* meal that tasted more like something ordered *à la carte* in Japan. As I scowled over my meal, a woman walked in who looked like a cross between a European and a savage, and she beckoned for me to come over, as if I were a child. The situation scared me a bit, so I decided to make my escape.

But the moment I stepped out on the street, a similar sort of woman accosted me.

"So, are you interested?" she asked.

A bit later, on the corner in front of my hotel, a woman charged between two people to grab my arm and then walked alongside me as she chattered about something. The only thing I could make out was that she was willing to "do it" for five francs.

I may have fled that neighborhood because of the police, but these women eager for five francs were at least as terrifying.

Later, after moving to a hotel on a main boulevard in the heart of Paris, I would stroll around in the evenings. Once I gave in to the temptation and entered a large café. The coffee was superb, so I ordered a second and then a third cup. And when I asked the garçon to bring me yet another, I noticed that a beautiful woman sitting five or so tables away was staring at me, laughing. She was a real beauty: a European type that you never have the chance to see in Japan.

I assumed she found my prodigious coffee consumption amusing, or maybe she was laughing to see such a strange, swarthy savage. Whatever it was, it made me feel uncomfortable. I even blushed a little, and looked away.

But in that other direction, another beautiful young woman was looking at me and laughing. I found it all somewhat vexing yet summoned the courage to stare back at her. I could see that she was not laughing but eager to say something to me, or so it seemed from the way she was moving her eyes and mouth.

Thinking this all a bit odd, I looked back at the first woman, who was in fact laughing. She was even more intent on talking to me, making exaggerated facial movements to communicate.

The situation was getting embarrassing so I quickly finished my coffee and left.

III

The next afternoon I had some business to attend to and hailed a taxi to reach my destination. The cars stopped frequently in the traffic-clogged streets, and then the stream of vehicles would move again, no faster than a person might walk. I cursed myself for taking a taxi when I was in a hurry.

When the taxi came to a rotary and was waiting to merge with traffic, I spied another pretty young woman who was laughing as she looked my way. Through the open car window I could hear that she was saying something, but when I leaned to listen more closely the taxi drove on.

The same day I splurged on dinner, spending thirty francs, and then promenaded on the boulevard. I came across some sort of musical-comedy act, with a young a woman singing a song about someone or another. I was pleased that I could more or less follow the song and story, but the jokes were so daft that I soon got bored and walked on.

I strolled past the bright shop windows and the terraces of the sidewalk cafés, where flocks of men and women were seated around the outdoor tables, enjoying conversations over their drinks. Here and there a woman sat by herself, flashing her eyes at a solitary man or smiling at someone passing by.

Almost all of the women walking along flashed a look at men passing in the opposite direction. But just when you thought that the look had some meaning, you might notice she was holding hands with someone else or had an arm around the man she was chattering with.

The women all had beautiful white skin or powdered faces with rouge; wore red lipstick and black eyeliner; and were adorned with hats and clothing of all colors.

They looked magnificent from behind: tall and slender, accentuated by the long coats they were wearing that time of year. The heels of the tall boots that covered the women's small feet struck the pavement with a resounding sound as they walked along, their hips swaying back and forth.

In my state of rapture I bumped into one woman; or I should say she ran into me, quite deliberately.

"Hi there. Wanna have some fun with me tonight?" she asked, with a tilt of her head, in a cute voice, delicate but crisp.

It wasn't an unpleasant encounter, but I scampered away, feeling a bit under siege, and rushed into what looked like another musical-comedy show.

I opened the door and stepped inside, but was somewhat

surprised to find no place to buy a ticket. An usher came up to me to ask:

"Shall I show you to a good seat, sir?"

"Ah . . . yes. The best seat you have," I said rather grandiosely, not knowing how much it would cost me.

Another door opened, revealing a spacious dance stage. I was led past a lively orchestra to a table near the front, while a dozen women on stage kept at their dancing. I handed a two-franc tip to the usher, who thanked me earnestly and whispered something in a low voice that I couldn't make out. When I asked him to repeat it, he said:

"If a girl catches your eye just let me know; I'll call her over for you." Then he placed a small sheet on the table.

Another man came over with a large menu listing the champagnes available. The prices, which were between fifty and sixty francs, alarmed me. And I noticed what was written on the smaller sheet: Entrance Free of Charge. Drinks Mandatory.

What have I gotten myself into, I thought.

I brushed aside the waiter, pretending to be engrossed in the dancing. The women on stage pulled up the short hems of their skirts and lifted their legs high into the air. Once they had finished their dance, other men and women in the performance crowded the stage and began dancing. Taking this as my opportunity, I dashed out of the place before the waiter came for my order.

IV

Today in Paris the *midinettes* are on strike. You won't find the word in the dictionary; it's Parisian slang to refer to the working women who file out from the shops and factories at noon (*midi*) to grab a bite to eat. I was told that these women do other work on their lunch breaks apart from their regular jobs. That explanation helped me memorize the word.

The *midinettes* on strike are the seamstresses; eight thousand of them went out on strike for four hours. The women demonstrated on a major thoroughfare and invited workers from other factories to join the strike. Here and there the demonstrators clashed with police.

I met one of the striking women and asked about her situation. Still young and not yet skilled at her job, she only earned sixty francs a week. The average for most of the *midinettes* was fifty or sixty francs a week, for a monthly wage of around four hundred francs. Most of the poor married women of Paris and their daughters were in this situation.

The woman I talked to jotted down for me her daily expenditures:

Breakfast (coffee and bread)	0.60
Train fare (round trip)	0.35
Lunch	4.50
Dinner	3.50
Laundry	0.80

Rent..2.00
Other (for illness or entertainment)........2.00
Clothing..2.00

Daily total 15.75
Weekly total 110.25
Monthly total 441.00
Yearly total 5,292.00
Yearly income 3,120.00

Yearly deficit......................2,172.00 francs

She ate lunch (or more like a mid-afternoon snack) with friends; splurging occasionally for a glass of wine. Such women rented an attic room in a cheap hotel for two francs a night. Very few of the *midinettes* in Paris lived with their parents; most stayed in those cheap attic rooms.

The problem for the women was how to make up the yearly deficit of two thousand francs. Some cooked their own meals and only ate bread and potatoes for lunch and dinner; others tightened their belts when it came to laundry, entertainment, and clothing; some moved in with boyfriends so both could save money; and then there were those who worked during their lunch breaks, the *midinettes*.

The Times of London mocked the *midinettes*, suggesting that they went out on strike because the cost of silk stockings and cosmetics had gone up. It's true that quite a few women walk around Paris in silk stockings and make-up, but you also see many who don't fit that description. In any case, most of

The Toilets of Paris

the *midinettes* who wear stockings and make-up are forced to do so by the shop owners who employ them.

The striking women, with collection boxes hanging from their necks, walked around to the cafés to gather funds and were subjected to teasing remarks from the "gentlemen" seated there. Things like:

"Why not do some streetwalking for me, instead?"

Some of the women did in fact take up streetwalking, and even turn it into their main occupation—making it impossible for the *midinettes* to win higher wages.

The beautiful young women could only maintain the looks needed to work the streets and dawdle in the cafés by avoiding childbirth by any means. Amid the steadily rising prices, poor women hoping to survive, whether they looked like ladies or beggars, had to avoid the burden of children. There was a noticeable trend in France toward fewer births, as reflected in recent statistics.

Last year, 1922, the number of births was around 759,000; a decrease of about 20,000 compared to the previous year and 53,000 or so fewer than the year before that. Here are the statistics in more detail for 1922:

```
Births ..........................................759,846
Deaths..........................................689,267
Births over deaths.....................................70,579
```

Compare this to the births over deaths for the two preceding years:

    1921 117,023
    1920 159,790

The number of deaths has also decreased slightly, mainly due to premature deaths, particularly among children of the poor. The statistics also show a decline in the number of marriages:

    1920 623,869
    1921 456,211
    1922 383,220

Here are the statistics on the number of marriages per 10,000 people:

    1922 195
    1921 233
    1920 318

Birth control presents a problem for the poor. The diaphragms recommended by Margaret Sanger cost fifty francs a piece, even though they cannot be used for very long. And that gourd-shaped bidet I described earlier is something that no poor woman could hope to own. Workers tend to have many children. I know some workers with five or six, or as many as seven or eight; but most of these children die in infancy or early childhood. Even many of those disreputable women seen strolling the streets have had a child before turning twenty.

That's the reason why the toilets need to be wide enough

for an infant's head to pass through easily. For a fee of about five hundred francs a doctor will perform an abortion in secret, but that's far too expensive for a poor woman.

Abortion is a felony in France. But a few days ago I read in a newspaper article that there's now talk of making it a misdemeanor. Every year a number of people are charged with the crime, although I don't recall the exact figure mentioned in the article.

Changing the law in France would seem a welcome reform for the poor, but that's not necessarily the case. Precisely because abortion has been a felony up to now, many jurors have had sympathy for the accused and been reluctant to cast a guilty verdict. And even when the accused is found guilty, the sentence is not always carried out. If the law is changed to make abortion a misdemeanor, there may no longer be trial by jury in such cases and judges would be less sympathetic. And that seems to be the very reason why the reform was proposed.

April 30, 1923 – Paris

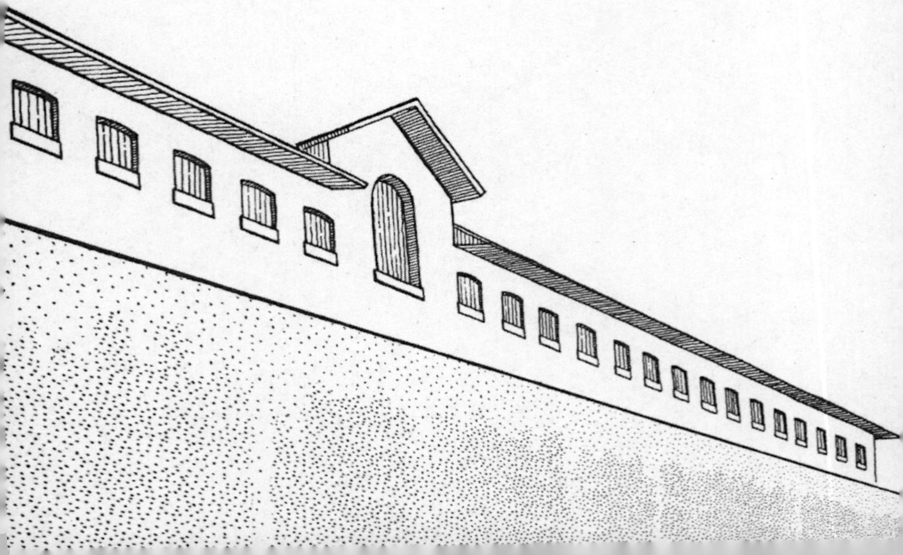

Prison Songs

I

Two things I like
About Paris:
No women to get out of trouble
And this prison wine and tobacco

A LOUSY SPEECH is sure to be prefaced by a long-winded apology. The same is true for a poem. First there is the preamble to the prologue, followed by the lengthy prologue itself.

"No women to get out of trouble" refers to the topic raised in "The Toilets of Paris"; but there my account turned into a sort essay—and a bit stodgy as a result. The "I" narrating that section would seem a type who is always fleeing from loose women.

But that is just the appearance, quite contrary to the reality.

My Escapes from Japan

Far from running the other way, more often than not I was the one in pursuit.

One woman I chased after was a dancer named Dolly. She worked at the famous, but not very elegant, Bal Tabarin, a cabaret known to any foreigner who has visited Paris. I picked her out from among the dancers there, not that it's anything to brag about.

In Paris I was staying at a hotel* near that dance hall. But, in the middle of March, I reluctantly had to leave the city, which seemed to be getting too dangerous for me. I escaped to Lyon to prepare for my trip to Germany.

I needed an exit permit from police headquarters in Lyon before I could obtain a visa from the German consulate. On each visit to the police I was told the permit would be issued on the next day or the day after. In this way, more than a month was frittered away. Irritated and missing Paris as May Day approached, I decided to go back to the city and have a quick look around.

On the evening after my arrival in Paris I planned to visit the area near place de l'Opéra and have dinner there, leaving enough time to visit Dolly later. But while dining in that neighborhood at the Grand Café, I ran into a woman with whom I'd once had a bit of fun but for some reason never met for a second date. We hadn't seen each other since then, but now she had me cornered.

The next day was May Day, and I was eager to meet Dolly that evening. But this time I was cornered by a more daunting

---

* Hôtel Victor Masse.

Prison Songs

adversary—the Paris police.

The charges against me had all sorts of names: Disturbing the peace; Resisting a government official; Violating passport regulations. I had to spend the night at a police station, the next night at police headquarters, and the third day found me in a detention cell at La Santé Prison.

My prison stay, however, turned out to be carefree. I could lie in bed all day, blowing smoke rings; a bottle of beer or wine on the table; there was nothing for me to do but take it easy.

Later I'll say a bit more about my drinking habits, but first a short poem dedicated to Dolly:

> In my solitary cell
> Lying on the sofa
> Smoke from a cigar
> And thoughts of Dolly
> My ballet dancer

Spring was outside my cell window. I could smell the new leaves on the chestnut trees lining the boulevard just outside the tall prison wall. With little else to do, I lounged on the bed, looking out on the fresh, almost transparent green leaves. As the ash fell from my cigar, the room filled with pale purple smoke that looked to me like my dancing Dolly, for often she wore a lavender dress on stage that suited her so well.

My Escapes from Japan

II

The souvenir of my prison stay:
The memory
Of the taste of wine
Ça va, ça va!

For five or six years now my doctor has been telling me that I should drink a bit of alcohol for my health.

I always found it impossible to follow that advice. After a couple sips of sake, I turn bright red, straight to my fingertips, and my heart starts pounding like a drum. A bite or two of an alcohol-pickled vegetable has the same effect. Even with cider, two cups would be enough to turn me into a raving lunatic.

Whiskey, I had heard, is the most delightful of drinks, so I tried putting a teaspoon in my black tea every day, but even that tiny dose made me wretch.

Since coming to France, or I should say since embarking from Shanghai on a French ship, a bottle of wine has accompanied each meal. I tried drinking some once, but found it so bitter that I never gave the bottle a second glance thereafter.

In prison, though, I noticed that wine and beer were among the items allowed inmates. In a fit of boredom, I decided to try to build up a tolerance to one or the other. Beer, I found, was too bitter and red wine too harsh, but white wine seemed like something I could manage. If a child can gulp back a cup of tea, it seemed I should be able to down a bit of wine. So one day I asked for a bottle of white wine with my meal. And I didn't find it all that disagreeable; hence the *Ca va, ca va!* in that short poem.

> It tasted bitter yesterday
> But sweeter today,
> This *vin blanc*
> I'm beginning to like

The *vin blanc* was still rather bitter for my taste, but by taking little sips, as if it were medicine, I managed to drink it. Stretched out on my bed, I enjoyably filled the free moments of the day sipping the white wine that got me a bit flushed.

> My great feat:
> Drinking a bottle
> Of *vin blanc*
> Every two days

The "bottle" was just a *demi*, though, half or a quarter the size of a regular bottle.

On the day of my release from prison, after twenty-four days in detention, I polished off an entire *demi* while waiting for the deportation forms to be filled out at the Police des Étrangers division of police headquarters, surrounded by close to a hundred detectives.

> The taste of each

My Escapes from Japan

Evening drink
Will bring back
Memories of that Paris prison

I resolved to have a good swig of white wine every evening after returning to Japan.

III

Sipping my *vin blanc*
Caught up in a poem
A spring day
A spring feeling

Spring filled my mind, but there was nothing romantic about that feeling. In my cell I was more like a saint. Occasionally my thoughts did drift to Dolly, with whom I'd slept—but that's all we'd done, only slept next to each other.

Faire l'amour, ce n'est pas tout.
Tu es trop jolie pour cela. Je t'adore.

Those were the sugary lines (too sweet for me to write down in Japanese) that I repeated to Dolly like a lullaby until she drifted off to sleep.

Perhaps this was why I thought of Dolly from time to time. There were women with whom I really *had* slept: one woman in Lyon; another who escorted me to a train depot late one

Prison Songs

night; that woman I met on the eve of May Day; and another nicknamed "Chapeau Rouge" for her habit of always wearing a red hat. But the memory of these women never came to mind.

No, there was nothing romantic about how I felt; just a simple feeling of spring, tranquil and easy-going. Ordinarily I'm so busy, dealing with all sorts of people, so to find myself alone in prison, without any real worries, was simply magnificent. I wouldn't have felt that way if my sentence had been too long or if I had been jailed too often. But this time, with spring in the air, my prison mood was sublime. And sipping my *vin blanc* made the feeling all the more delectable. I had the desire to write poetry, however bad, and indulge in my carefree thoughts.

It was only just after my release from prison that friends in Japan learned from the newspapers of my arrest. I regret that they didn't know just how tranquil my prison stay had been.

Other inmates at La Santé Prison during my stay included the French Communist Party leader Cachin[*] and a dozen or so of his comrades, all arrested at the time the crisis broke out over the occupation of the Ruhr valley. They included two German communists, one of whom was a parliamentary representative or something of the sort. I was still on the ship heading to France at the time all of these communists were arrested.

---

[*] Marcel Cachin (1869–1958); a founding member of the French Communist Party. Editor of the party's newspaper, *l'Humanité*, from 1918 to 1958.

My Escapes from Japan

After I was sentenced to La Santé, Cachin and the other French communists were released on bail, but the two Germans were kept in prison. Under French law there were no grounds to keep them, but the two remained locked up anyway for purely political reasons. Enraged to still be behind bars after the others had been let go, the Germans went on a hunger strike to demand immediate release. After hearing of this, a handful of anarchists among the political prisoners began their own hunger strike in solidarity.

For about ten days the Germans had nothing to eat or drink. They were nearly dead by the time the prison transferred them to a hospital, from where they were eventually set free two or three days after my own release.

I could speculate on what I might have done had I learned sooner of their hunger strike, but it's too embarrassing to engage in such idle talk.

July 11, 1923 – Aboard the Hakone Maru

Prison Life until Deportation

I

I HAD ANTICIPATED that my overseas itinerary would include a stopover in prison at some point, and in Paris that moment finally arrived.

*

Getting locked up is nothing new for me. But I hadn't expected it to happen in Paris.

In Japan before my departure I didn't have the chance to meet anyone just back from Europe, but in China I did encounter several people who had returned from France. They all reassured me that once I crossed over into France everything would be fine.

My Escapes from Japan

I learned from them that even without a passport I wouldn't be stopped en route or when I disembarked in Marseille.

I happened to have a rather good fake passport. The nationality and name listed were not mine, but the photograph was of me, wearing the same clothes I had brought for the trip. I felt confident that the authorities would not spot it as a fake. And in fact the French consulate and the English consulate each issued me a visa right away on its basis. After all the trouble I had gone through to get that passport, I did not plan to cross the border without showing it.

My worries during the voyage had been directed to other matters; ones that could not be solved beforehand. And any mistake on that count would have left me no choice but to abandon the trip.

But everything went smoothly in the end, and I felt, as I had back in Japan, that once I crossed over into France my problems would be behind me.

This expectation seemed to have been confirmed when I went to get my visa at the French consulate. I handed over my passport to the clerk and, just when I thought he was taking it somewhere else, he came back and issued me a visa as soon as I paid the handling fee. The rather indifferent way he carried out the transaction surprised me.

On my way to France I heard a lot about how free the country was.

"Wait until you get to France, then you'll know what freedom is all about."

That's a line I recall from a conversation I had with "Madame N.," a former student at Moscow University who spent

Prison Life until Deportation

several years studying in Paris. She had been forced to leave Russia when her brother's connection to the Social Revolutionary Party made her suspect in the eyes of the Czarist bureaucracy. Later she spent quite some time in Japan. We happened to be traveling to France on the same ship.

"When you first arrive at a hotel in France, be sure to present your business card, whether genuine or a fake," she advised me. "As long as you show someone your card, you won't get any other questions. That would never work in Japan or Russia, of course."

*

But soon after we disembarked in Marseille, Madame N. had an experience at a hotel that punctured her belief in French freedom. The man at the front desk pulled out a type-written form that he asked us to fill in. A closer look revealed it was a detailed register, requiring far more information than those in Japan.

After exchanging glances, Madame N. and I each filled in the information until we came to the part that asked us to list our *carte d'identité*.

"What's this all about?" I asked her.

"I was wondering the same thing," she said, laying down her pen for a moment.

"If you don't have your *carte d'identité*, a passport is fine," the clerk told us. I wasn't sure what he meant at first, but then realized I could just write down my passport number. Afterwards, the man then led us up to a room on the second floor.

My Escapes from Japan

This one little altercation clouded Madame N.'s expression, although neither of us yet knew what a *carte d'identité* was.

(I wrote in "Escaping Japan" that my first encounter with the carte d'identité *was in Paris, but that was only because I didn't want readers to know at the time where I entered France and what were my reasons for going there.)*

The next day Madame N. and I bid each other farewell. *(And now it is safe for me to say that I arrived in Marseille on February 13, after having departing Shanghai on January 5 on the "André Lebon.")*

I went to Lyon, where there were a number of comrades of the same nationality listed on my passport. I was carrying letters of introduction to them from the comrades in Shanghai. I wanted to make sure that I didn't cause the Lyon comrades any trouble, since I was traveling in Europe under the same nationality.

Anxious to be on my way to Paris, I told the comrades that I wanted to depart Lyon in a night or two but could come back to spend more time with them later. They advised me, however, to stay.

"It's more convenient here, with so many of us around," one of them said. "Set up residence in Lyon and get your *carte d'identité*, then you can travel wherever you like.'"

I was on a visa that only allowed me to travel from China to France; a separate visa was required to visit any other European country. I was also required to have a *carte d'identité*,

---

* Ōsugi stayed at 37 chemin de l'Étoile d'Alaï, in the west of Lyon, according to French police records.

Prison Life until Deportation

which any foreigner residing in France for more than two weeks had to obtain from the police. Without this identification listing one's place of residence, a foreigner risked arrest at any time, as well as a prison sentence and deportation if there was no valid reason for not having it.

"It's basically a dog collar," one comrade (whom I'll call "A.") said, pulling out of a pocket his own identification papers with a photograph attached. The document required two French guarantors and two others from your home country, and even the birthdate of both parents.

The process of obtaining the *carte d'identité* generally takes a week. During my wait I had hoped to attend a meeting of some French comrades that I read about in the newspaper. But when I asked the Chinese comrades to accompany me, comrade A. and the others refused. They explained that I would be taken into immediate custody if I attended the meeting, not only ending my chance of getting a *carte d'identité* but making it impossible to obtain a passport to travel in Europe—and perhaps even placing myself in peril.

*

Those experiences gave me a clear sense of the political reaction that had settled upon France after the war. Far from being a safe haven, the country seemed fraught with dangers flickering in front of my eyes.

My Escapes from Japan

II

The *carte d'identité* was shaped like a pocket-size notebook. On the back page was a space for listing information on departures, arrivals, and repatriation. Whenever you departed your place of residence, you had to visit the police to have this page stamped.

Ignoring that rigmarole, I headed straight to Paris to visit l'Union anarchiste, whose office in Belleville was under heavy surveillance (as I described in "Escaping Japan").

When I checked into a hotel near the office, the proprietor asked me not only to sign the hotel register but also to show my *carte d'identité*.

These bureaucratic hassles were making me feel more ill at ease. I decided to visit some other Chinese comrades on the outskirts of Paris and further out in the countryside, joined by the Chinese comrade* who had accompanied me from Lyon. After a few days, the two of us returned to the hotel in Belleville that an Italian comrade had introduced to me. This comrade had been staying at the hotel herself, but we returned to find her making hasty preparations to move on to another place. She told us that the intrusive police presence was driving her away.

The Chinese comrade chose to head back to Lyon right

---

* Shō Keishū (Japanese reading of his name); one of the Chinese delegates chosen to attend the planned anarchist congress in Berlin.

Prison Life until Deportation

away. And I decided to find a safer place myself, relying on the Italian comrade for help. That evening the two of us went to the headquarters of the CGTU* to attend a popular musical concert hosted by *le Libertaire*, only to find almost a dozen uniformed policemen standing guard outside.

On the following day, when I visited the Libertaire office, I encountered an emaciated man with a shaggy beard and long hair. He was on the verge of collapse and could barely speak. We learned that he was a comrade from Hungary who had been thrown in prison there for six months because of his anti-militarist activities. Just after his release the man fled secretly to France, but there he was arrested again for lacking a passport. The day we saw him he had been released after three months in prison and was about to be deported.

That same evening I visited a young Russian comrade whom I had been planning to meet for some time. There was no reply at his apartment, though, even after I knocked on the door several times. I thought he must be out, but when I gave the door once last knock a trembling voice inside told me to wait a moment. Finally, the door opened and the comrade plunged into my arms after recognizing my face. When I asked what was wrong, he said that he had been bracing himself for arrest, certain the police had arrived. He had no passport and had fled Russia to Germany, and from there to France.

---

* The CGTU (Confédération générale du travail unitaire) was a Communist-led labor union formed in 1922 out of a split within the CGT (Confédération générale du travail).

My Escapes from Japan

The comrade told me he was heading straight back to Germany. It made me realize that in a country as vigilant as France I had little choice but to hide out. The situation seemed somewhat better in Germany, so I resolved to make my way there as soon as possible, especially since the international anarchist congress was supposed to convene in Berlin on the first of April. I was willing to risk arrest at the congress, where I would have to reveal my real identity, but did not want the authorities to get hold of me before then.

It was around this time that my Japanese friend S.[*] paid me a visit. My strict policy since leaving Japan for France had been to avoid contact with other Japanese, but I made an exception for S. and told him confidentially that I was in Paris and where I was staying.

Once S. had been apprised of my situation, he suggested that we find a new place to stay together, since he had decided to return to Paris from the countryside. He went out to look for a suitable hotel, and we ended up staying at the place he found.

"Since you can't risk going to any political gatherings or visiting many people, we might as well set up camp in the city's biggest playground," he suggested.

That was our reason for choosing a hotel right in the heart of Montmartre. And we proceeded, as planned, to enjoy ourselves day and night. During this time, I was awaiting word

---

[*] Hayashi Shizue (1895–1945); a painter and friend of Ōsugi's from anarcho-syndicalist circles in Tokyo. Resided in France and Germany from 1921 to 1926.

Prison Life until Deportation

from the Lyon comrades, who were to notify me as soon as a new visa was issued that would allow me to travel elsewhere in Europe. The plan called for me to then return to Lyon and prepare straight away for departure to Germany.

A week or so later, just as I was settling into my new life of pleasure and the fun was getting underway, a message did arrive from Lyon, but it coincided with some rather alarming news. I learned that the Japanese government had wired its embassy in Paris to order an immediate investigation into the conduct of S. And I took it for granted that the investigation would turn up my own whereabouts as well.

(I overheard this rumor a couple days before May Day but later learned that the Japanese government had, by that time, already ordered its embassy in Germany to search for me and sent the same directive to other embassies and consulates in Europe.)

S. and I had used up our money by then, but we managed to borrow a bit more and beat a hasty retreat from Paris.

*

S. returned to his old place in the countryside, and I went back to Lyon. At police headquarters there, I requested permission to travel to Germany, making no mention of all the other places I had visited in France. Until I received that permission, it was pointless to request a visa at the German consulate.

The office of the Police des Étrangers, which issues visas, was located in an old courthouse building, a bit removed from police headquarters. The officials there told me it would take four or five days to handle the paperwork, and that if I stopped by the same day the following week everything would certainly be ready. With the matter apparently settled, I fixed my departure date and got my preparations fully in order. While waiting, I read through a few recently published books on Germany and recited passages from a German primer. I even bought a book to learn Italian, since my plans included a stopover in Austria, Switzerland, and Italy on my return.

But on the awaited day, a week later, the officials informed me that my papers were still with the passport section, also located in the courthouse building. An official there told me that my papers had been passed along to Sûreté Générale, the investigative branch located in the same building. But when I went to their office, once again I was told to wait a couple more days until notified. It was all terribly annoying, but my only choice was to await that notification.

A couple days went by with no word. By the fourth day I had lost all patience and went to find out what was happening. I was told that the notification had been mailed the same day, and that I should return with it tomorrow.

On the following day, the Sûreté Générale officials investigated various points. First they asked me about obvious things that should have been clear from the passport and identification I presented for my application. Then they set about prying into every sort of detail regarding my activities since arriving France and the purpose of my trip to Germany. I answered the questions more or less coherently, but my biggest problem was that they also examined the details on my identification card. My parents' names and dates of birth were

Prison Life until Deportation

all fabrications, as was the information on the two guarantors in the country. Keeping track of all these lies was not easy, but somehow I managed.

What I did *not* manage was to find out when I could receive the permit for which I had applied. First they told me to return in two days, but when I did the message became, "Come back on the day after tomorrow." I did as I was told, thinking it would surely be ready this time around, but again was asked to wait another day. The next day it was "the day after tomorrow" and so on like this, as each time I was asked to wait another day or two.

The police checked up on the proprietor of the place where I was staying three or four times and also looked into various matters regarding S., who had spent a night there, too.

Feeling increasingly nervous, I considered giving up on the legal procedures and just crossing the border clandestinely, as my Russian comrade had done. Since arriving in France, I had debated the Lyon comrades over this issue of legality. My view from the start had been that it was better to dispense with the bothersome *carte d'identité* and just travel around as I liked. But I reluctantly went along with their above-board approach, not wanting to create trouble for these comrades who had taken care of me. And now, once again, I was playing by the rules.

That's why I spent an unpleasant and worrisome month and a half of stopping by police headquarters almost every day.

My Escapes from Japan

III

I was fed up with waiting.

The congress had been postponed again. The basic plan now was to convene it in August, rather than the first of April, but it was not clear whether it would ever be held. The German comrades were saying that it was impossible to gather in Berlin. Some other place in Europe had to be found. But where? Some suggested Vienna, but that was also thought too risky.

As my time was being frittered away, my money also ran out. To make matters worse, I caught a cold and the medicine I took for it did my stomach in. Without even a centime, I spent a week in bed, barely eating anything.

Around the time I finally roused myself from bed some unexpected money arrived. It was also time for my regular bureaucratic appointment in Lyon. I was proving no match for the officials' way of putting me off another day or two with some excuse and the customary French shrug, always claiming to have no precise knowledge of the matter. The slight shrug and smirk annoyed me to no end. I invariably returned from such visits in a foul temper.

Spring had arrived in the meantime. Each day new leaves appeared on the chestnut and sycamore trees that lined the streets of the hilly suburb where I was staying. The colors were light green, with none of the darker colors mixed in that you see in Japan. Interspersed among the trees were red and white patches from the pear and cherry blossoms, and in between the branches I could see the reddish-orange roofs and walls of the houses on the other side. Everything was so bright and buoyant, almost unnervingly delicate, but the scene failed to raise my spirits.

And the rain kept falling down.

May Day was approaching. I had more or less given up on traveling to Germany. I decided to quietly make my way to Paris to see for myself what May Day was like in the city and check up on the month-old *midinette* seamstress strike. I also was keen to attend the sorts of meetings that I had been avoiding until then and gather some needed research materials. Plus I wanted to see the tree-lined streets of Paris in their spring foliage and observe the faces of the Parisian women.

*

On the evening of April 28 I departed Lyon, only telling one comrade where I was headed. Upon arriving in Paris I stopped by the Libertaire office to see Colomer. We promised to meet again at the May Day gathering in Saint Denis.

The authorities had banned outdoor meetings and demonstrations on May Day, and the workers had no plans to hold such activities in defiance of the ban. Communist politicos and CGTU leaders were careful not to rock the boat, fearing a clash with the police.

Even the plans for indoor meetings were limited. As far as I could tell, the only major gathering in the center of Paris was to be held at CGTU headquarters. All of the other events were planned for suburban working-class districts. A scheduled march to the American embassy to protest the death sentence handed down to Sacco and Vanzetti, our Italian comrades, was also moved outside the city at the insistence of the communists.

The May Day meeting in Saint Denis was expected to draw a crowd. This suburb north of Paris, a center of iron production, was known for its revolutionary minded workers. Colomer was to address the meeting in Saint Denis as the anarchists' representative.

I headed out early on the first of May to get a feel for the atmosphere in the city. What I encountered was just an ordinary day, more or less, only a bit more forlorn than usual, with not a taxi in sight.* All of the shops were open. The trains and subway cars still ran, packed with workers who were slightly better dressed than usual and accompanied by their wives and children. To my eye they certainly did not seem to be on their way to a May Day gathering on the city outskirts.

"Hey there, it's May Day, *no?*" I asked a worker next to me, using the working-class argot I had picked up. "Where are you off to?"

"Ah, thanks to the holiday we're going out to the countryside," the man answered breezily, one hand around the waist of his not very attractive wife, the other gripping a basket full of sandwiches and wine.

I had to clench my fists to resist the urge to box the man across the ears.

The May Day handbills of the CGTU plastered on the

---

* Paris taxi drivers were on strike that day.

Prison Life until Deportation

walls were all torn or peeling off. Next to some were CGT handbills bearing the warning that, "May Day participants are German spies!"

*

The doors to the workers' hall in Saint Denis* opened at three in the afternoon, and soon it was nearly bursting with more than eight hundred workers.

The speeches began. The scheduled speakers took to the podium, one after another, delivering long, grandiloquent speeches that touched on the slogans of the day: End the Ruhr occupation; Down with war; Amnesty for wartime political prisoners; Worker solidarity. The applause began to wane; yawning faces could be seen. More than a few even exited the hall.

Occasional shouts could be heard from the crowd: "Enough talk! Everyone, outside!" The shouts were coming from the anarchists who had been hawking *le Libertaire* and *la Revue anarchiste* outside the hall. But no one else was echoing the call. And often someone from the stage would descend into the crowd to stifle the protest.

Colomer and I had planned to head off somewhere for a meeting after his speech, but it all seemed rather pointless by then. My only desire was to get behind the podium and urge the crowd to go outside.

---

* The meeting apparently was held at a domed, two-story building on rue Légion d'honneur, facing the Basilica Cathedral.

My Escapes from Japan

Right before Colomer rose to give his speech I called him over to ask if I might briefly address the hall after he had finished. He conveyed my request to the chairman (probably a Communist Party official), who came over to find out what I wanted to say. I knew that whenever communists and anarchists participated in the same event, each speaker had to promise what would be said in the speech. I told the chairman that I wanted to say a word about May Day in Japan. He had no idea of my name or who I was exactly, since Colomer had simply introduced me as a "syndicalist."

While Colomer was giving his speech, I jotted down notes for my own address, then took my place on the platform as he was wrapping up. Colomer said something about Germaine Berton, the female anarchist who had assassinated a royalist she thought responsible for the Ruhr occupation. And this brought out encouraging cries of *C'est ça, C'est ça!* from a teary-eyed woman near the stage who was around forty years old and looked like a worker.

My own speech, as I had promised the chairman, described May Day in Japan.

"The history of May Day in Japan doesn't go back very far," I began. "And not many workers participate yet. But Japanese workers all know about May Day. It's not celebrated on the outskirts of Tokyo but right in the city center. And it's not held inside, with speeches delivered in a hall, but outside, with demonstrations in the parks and public squares. May Day in Japan is not some sort of festival. ×××××. ××××××××××××××××××××××××××××."

Prison Life until Deportation

"××××××× fly out. ××××××× shine."*

My somewhat exaggerated explanation of May Day in Japan lasted twenty or thirty minutes, interspersed by the sight and sound of the woman near the stage, urging me on with her cry of *C'est ça, C'est ça!*

*

I stepped down from the platform—amid shouts of *Dehors! Dehors!*—and was trying to make my way outside when I was confronted by a handful of plainclothes cops who ordered me to come with them.

IV

Soon policemen had surrounded me. Without much trouble they seized my arms and legs and began to drag me away.

Not too long after, at the police station where I was taken, I could hear a crowd out front singing "The Internationale" and shouting. A herd of policemen who had been lurking in the courtyard of the station sprang into action to confront the crowd as I was taken away, further into the building.

(I later learned that around a dozen men and women at the hall in Saint Denis had tried to wrest back from the police the person they only knew as the "Japanese comrade." Workers also clashed

---

* Interspersed in the redacted text are the words *tobu* (fly out) and *hikaru* (shine), but the intended meaning is unclear.

with the police in front of the station where I was held, and were showered with kicks and blows by the police. By the end of the fight, a hundred or so workers were said to have been arrested.* Even from inside the station I could hear the sound of the struggle and of angry shouting.)

I didn't reveal my name or nationality to the police, and insisted that I had no passport or identification. Their other questions also yielded scant response from me.

Colomer soon arrived in the hope of securing my release. He advised me to tell the police the name[†] printed on my passport. The chairman of the gathering arrived not long after with a couple others. All agreed that the matter was trivial, and that I would be released if I just told the police my name.

Waiting for the right opportunity, I took a small notebook out of my pocket and slipped it into the chairman's hands. The notebook had been taken from me by the police, but in the commotion that followed the entrance of the chairman and his comrades I had managed to pocket it again. When my interrogation began a plainclothesman realized the notebook was gone and accused me of taking it. I stubbornly insisted that I didn't know what he was talking about. Another chimed in that he had seen me hand something to *Monsieur* So-and-So (the chairman) and asked his partner if he should

---

* According to a May 2 article in *le Figaro*, a crowd of five to six hundred, led by two city councilmen, marched on the police station in Saint Denis, and in the clash that followed five policemen were seriously injured.

† Ōsugi's assumed name is listed as "Tung Chen Tang" in French police records.

Prison Life until Deportation

go retrieve it.

"He doesn't have it, eh? Must have slipped it to someone," the first cop said, somewhat resigned to never getting the object back. The other policeman, after raising some sort of objection, went off. A little while later he came back with the notebook in hand, much to the pleasure of his colleague, who started to flip through it.

If they examined every page thoroughly, somewhere they would uncover the false name I was using. Or at least they would come across things I had jotted down to remember some of the nonsense for my *carte d'identité* application, like the names and ages of my fictional parents. In any case, they were sure to come across all sorts of leads. My hope had been to tear up the notebook and flush it down the toilet—and with that aim in mind I had asked for a drink of water right after the police dragged me to the station. I was allowed to use the toilet a bit later, but a policeman came to check up on me when I was trying to get rid of some calling cards and other papers inside the notebook, leaving me still holding it.

Having no other option, although still thinking it too soon, I decided to follow everyone's advice and give the police my (false) name. I said I was XY from country YZ and that my passport and *carte d'identité* were at police headquarters in Lyon pending permission to travel to Germany, as was in fact the case. I told the police I was a journalist and described my politics as "syndicalist." As for why I had introduced myself as a Japanese at the meeting, I said that that I was familiar with Japan, having lived there for many years, and thought it would be more effective to claim citizenship if I was going to

My Escapes from Japan

talk about the country.

I thought they might let me go after I divulged these facts, but at this point the situation was out of my hands.

*

It was already evening by the time the initial investigation ended.

Once the plainclothes officer left the interrogation room, a handful of tough-looking uniformed cops appeared, slapped handcuffs on me and led me away.

I thought they were taking me to a jail cell, but instead they led me to the entrance, where a large delivery truck was waiting with around ten officers. Using excessive force, they threw me into the back of the truck, then the officers hopped in and the truck sped away.

It was pitch black inside the spacious cargo area in the back. I was sitting cross-legged in a corner, both hands bound, policemen clutching my arms and shoulders.

Occasionally I could see the faces of the cops from the glow of their cigarettes. They did not look very European to me—more like savages from a French colony in Africa or the offspring of French soldiers stationed there. They seemed tense, as if they had just come from a fight, and were shouting something I couldn't make out.

After a while the cop holding my shoulder began to poke me, growling like a bear. Seeing that things might get rough, I removed my glasses and placed them in my pocket. But when the cop in front of me saw that, he hissed like a fox and struck

Prison Life until Deportation

me in the face.

Along with the blows that rained down on me was a torrent of snarls—like a monkey, bear, or fox might make—interspersed with some French that sounded to my ears like:

"I'll kill this bastard!"

"Where does this Chink think he gets off."

"German lackey!"

One even went so far as to remove a pistol from a bag and jab me on the head with it, and then do the same with an unsheathed sword.

Not long after, though, the truck stopped, for we seemed to have reached our destination. Half of the policeman dragged me from the front, while the other half struck and kicked me from behind, forcing me into a building. I was still in Saint Denis, just at a different police station. The policemen took me to a spacious room near the entrance, where they again pounced on me, tearing off my necktie, belt, and shoelaces before throwing me into a cell at the back of the room. There, with my clothes still on, I fell into a deep sleep.

*

Early the next morning two detectives arrived to take me to police headquarters, this time in a regular automobile.

They interrogated me there throughout the day, asking the same sort of questions as the day before. When I kept quiet about the hotels where I had stayed in Paris, a few policemen ushered me into a car that took me to each of the hotels, where the proprietors identified me. The police had known everything all along, I discovered.

I was brought back to headquarters, where I found a large room had been prepared for me, next to the Police des Étrangers office. A man who seemed to be the section chief greeted me.

"Monsieur Ōsugi, if I am not mistaken?"

He'd hit the nail right on the head. If they knew this much, it would be easier just to tell them whatever else they needed to know.

The inspector left the room for a moment on some errand, and one of the plainclothes detectives from the car entered.

"You might be pleased to know that there was quite a May Day in Japan," he said, pointing to a short article in the Communist paper *l'Humanité*. Under the headline "Dozens Injured," was a one-column article on the incident involving me at Saint Denis.

The article made no mention of my real name. I found out later that the police discovered my identity after someone from the Japanese embassy or somewhere else inquired if the man referred to in the article might be me. I also learned at some point, although I can't remember when, that an official from Japan's Interior Ministry and from Hyōgo Prefecture had been sent to Paris to find me.

The plainclothes cop, still quite young, was kind to me in many ways. When the tobacco I'd purchased on the way there ran out, he handed over a pack of his own rather harsh French cigarettes. And he advised me that if deported on the border with Spain I should make my way to Barcelona, rather than Madrid, because I would find more comrades of my political

Prison Life until Deportation

persuasion there. He even looked up maps and train schedules to show me which way to go and how long it would take.

But a couple other plainclothes cops took turns watching me too, and one was a right bastard. I recall him saying something like:

"They must have paid you quite a lot for you to come all the way from Lyon to make a speech."

He drew very near me as he spoke and vulgarly fingered a large scar near his mouth, probably a war wound.

"You must have bought this in Germany, huh?" he said, handling a knife with a "Made in Sheffield" label that I had purchased in Singapore.

He kept on like this, picking over my belongings and implying that each had been bought in Germany. In his eyes, it was all proof of my guilt. He thought that the German government had paid me to stir up the workers in France.

"Look," I said to him at one point. "I'm not going to bother talking to anyone who spouts such nonsense."

This enraged him. "You Boche bastard!" he shouted, shaking an enormous fist in front of my face.

"If you're going to hit me, get on with it," I said out of irritation, and braced myself for the blow, but at that moment the friendlier detective entered and led my tormentor to another room.

Now that my real name was known, the investigation was easily concluded. Another detective took me to the fifth or sixth floor of a different building, where I was stripped to undergo a physical examination and be photographed.

In Japan the police were content to simply measure height

My Escapes from Japan

and weight and take a person's fingerprints. But the French, true to form, adopted a more scientific approach. Like anthropologists, they determined the size and length of my skull, and measured the length from my outstretched fingers to my forearm. A special chair was used for the mug shots, so that after the profile was taken it swiveled around easily for the frontal shot.

After all this had been done, I was escorted to another building for my preliminary hearing. Once this very cursory court proceeding was over, I was brought back to the same building as before and placed in a cell. All of my possessions were confiscated, but I was allowed cigarettes and matches.

I stretched out on the bed at once, admiring those two objects, and enjoyed a smoke before drifting off to sleep.

I must have been rather tired, but also it has long been my custom to lie down and sleep whenever I'm tossed into a jail or holding cell.

V

The next morning, the third of May, I was transported along with around fifteen comrades (?) to La Santé Prison in two large horse-drawn wagons.

La Santé is a detention center, famous for holding political prisoners. At some point on my voyage to France, I don't recall exactly where, I heard over the wireless from France that Cachin and a dozen other Communist Party leaders had been detained at the prison. I figured they might still be there.

Prison Life until Deportation

Soon after I arrived in France, a dozen or so anarchists were also sent to La Santé to join the other anarchists already there.

*

The guards brought me some more cigarettes and matches. Unlike in Japan, where each inmate carries back to his cell one of the futons laid out in the area where the six wings of the star-shaped prison intersect, at La Santé we were handed a dingy nightshirt and a hand towel of sorts.

Entering the prison put me in an inquisitive mood. As a guard led me down a wide corridor, I looked all around at my new surroundings.

He placed me in cell number 20, on the ground floor of holding block 10. The square cell was just around eight tatami mats in size,* with a large window that let in plenty of light. The window was some five feet wide at its base and about the same height, the top two feet arching into a semi-circle.

None of the hotels where I had stayed up to then, apart from a few elegant exceptions, had such a magnificent window. And it was all the more impressive considering that the base of the window only began at eye level.

Later, when I went out to the yard for exercise, I saw that the large windows were only on the ground floor, whereas the windows on the three floors above were just half the size.

From the window I could see the tall prison wall nearby and above it the branches of three chestnut trees, the white

---

* Roughly twelve by twelve feet.

My Escapes from Japan

flowers already in bloom.

To the left of this westward facing window was a small bed attached to the wall, covered with a woolen blanket. I sat down on the bed and found that its spring mattress made it quite comfortable, and the blanket was nicer than the one at my boarding house in Belleville.

To the right of the window was a table, also attached to the wall, with a proper wooden chair placed under it.

On the wall to the left of this table, near the entrance, were two hanging shelves on which a bowl, a wooden spoon and fork, and other utensils were placed.

And on that same wall, facing the entrance, there was a water spigot in the corner, near the foot of the bed, below which was the large opening of a white porcelain toilet. This was the only slightly irritating thing about the room, as it meant you had to wash dishes right above the toilet.

The floorboards were an imitation mosaic, the little pieces of wood placed in a rather stylish zigzag arrangement.

This must have been what Anatole France's fictional character Jerôme Crainquebille, a vegetable peddler arrested by the police, meant when he said that the floor of his prison cell was clean enough to eat off of. In Paris, I watched a moving picture[*] based on the novel, with a scene that showed Crainquebille just after he entered prison. I was struck by how happy he seemed as he looked around his prison cell.

I felt terribly fond of my own prison cell from the moment I set foot inside. After having a look around and trying out

---

[*] The 1922 silent film *Crainquebille*, directed by Jaques Feyder.

the springs on that comfortable bed, I stretched out and lit myself a cigarette.

*

After a while, a prison guard brought two half sheets of printed paper from the canteen and affixed them to the wall above my table. Under the heading "Provisions and prices" in large print was a column listing "Consumable goods" and another listing "Food," along with the price of each item.

All sorts of daily goods were available: ink, paper, pens, hairbrushes, toothbrushes, sponges, hair cream, towels, cigarettes and cigars, leaf tobacco, along with around twenty things to eat, including bread, steak, roast beef, sausage, omelets, ham, sardines, macaroni, salad, coffee, chocolate, butter, jam, sugar, salt, and rice, as well as various fruits and wine and beer.

Each week a menu was also handed out to inmates listing some of the rather tasty-looking selections available from the canteen for breakfast and dinner. And, if the servings were not sufficient, we were allowed to order extra dishes to supplement the evening meal.

Restrictions were placed on items available to convicted felons (although no one in my cell block had been convicted yet). For example, an inmate might only be allowed meat three times a week, or wine and beer consumption might be limited to sixty centiliters a day.

After looking at the lists posted on the wall, I knocked on the door to summon the guard and ordered some things. When I requested to have my meals brought every day, he asked:

"Do you want meals from our restaurant or from the outside?"

The guard looked like an ex-soldier, with a sturdy face and body, the smell of wine always on his breath; yet he seemed surprisingly fond of people. He spoke in a strange French accent that required my full attention to arrive at some understanding. I told him that I would prefer ordering from an outside restaurant, figuring it would taste better.

A bit later a young waiter from a restaurant outside the prison arrived to show me a small menu and take my lunch order. There were a dozen or so dishes on the menu. I chose four and made the extravagant request for the best white wine they had, and the waiter headed back to the restaurant with my order.

All of this had put me in a fine mood. It seemed that I would only need the equivalent of forty or fifty yen a month to enjoy quite a pleasant stay.

*

When the order arrived, I had a few sips of the wine and made short work of the food, even polishing off some chocolate for desert. Then I climbed back into bed and puffed away at a cigar. My thoughts turned back, not for the first time, to home.

Word of my arrest probably would have reached Japan by now through the newspaper wires. None of my acquaintances would be particularly surprised by the news, but the children—especially my eldest daughter, Mako—would no doubt be worried by the way the adults were acting, even if no mention of my arrest were made.

My wife told me in a letter that when Muraki,* who was staying at our house, was wrapping a book to send to someone, Mako asked him softly: "Aren't you going to send Daddy anything?" When we sent her off to stay at a friend's house so she wouldn't notice my departure, she was sure I was going to be arrested. Whenever Mako asked where I was, the response was either silence or a change of subject. Sometimes at night, alone with her mother, she would speak casually about the rumors surrounding me. Knowing what Mako must be feeling, I thought I should send her a telegram. I sat down at the table and wrote a number of simple messages, but did not come up with anything that could be sent inexpensively as a telegram. After those attempts, I jotted down an odd little thing:

Mako, sweet Mako!

Papa's now in La Santé
A world-famous
Prison in Paris

But don't worry, dear Mako
I feast on French meals
Savor chocolates
And puff-puff my cigars on the sofa

---

* Muraki Genjirō (see footnote on p. 3).

My Escapes from Japan

Cheer up Mako!
Thanks to this prison stay
Papa will soon be home

Just wait a little longer
You'll see me soon with my
Load of presents and kisses
For my baby girl

I took to reciting this jingle in a loud voice while lounging about my cell all day long. The strange thing was that, even though I wasn't the least bit sad, tears began to stream down my face when I chanted those lines. My voice trembled as the tears flowed.

*

I should mention that I did not always feast so well in La Santé. At first it seemed I would have more than enough money to spend two or three luxurious months in prison, having just received a payment from *Tokyo nichinichi shimbun* for a newspaper article[*] I wrote before my arrest. But near the end of the first week in jail, a guard informed me that I had little money left because most of it was seized by the court on the suspicion that it had been supplied by Germany.

This left me with no choice but to eat the standard prison

---

[*] "Toilets of Paris" (*Pari no benjo*).

Prison Life until Deportation

fare for the time being.

At around eight in the morning a loaf of black bread about the size of a child's head was slipped through the food slot of my cell. I could only manage a couple bites of this cold and crumbly, tasteless bread that was not just black but charred.

In all my time spent in the slums of Belleville, where I bought bread at a local bakery for the meals I cooked, I never once came across a loaf of black bread. And I doubted that anyone in Paris ate such stuff.

In the early afternoon the loud cry of "Soup!" could be heard in the prison. This soup, as it was called, was brought to us on a rattling cart. We were handed an aluminum bowl filled with slightly discolored hot water seasoned with salt. Beads of viscous oil glistened on the surface, while scraps of carrot and cabbage settled at the bottom of the bowl.

One look at this soup on my first day in prison was enough to know it wasn't for me.

A couple hours after the soup, another bowl of food was brought to us. There were stewed beans one day, and boiled potatoes on another. I liked beans and potatoes, so from the beginning I didn't turn them down. On a different day I was brought rice gruel with quite large pieces of meat mixed in. But the meat was so tough that I had to spit it out after a failed attempt to chew it. That gruel with rice was brought twice a week.

That was roughly the extent of the culinary delights in prison.

At first I could not get much of this food down, but my hunger drove me to manage eventually. By the end, I was able to wolf down a whole day's worth of black bread right after it was handed over to me, and polish off every bite of the afternoon bowls of food as well. But even so, I felt hungry. And they didn't bring me water, so I had to guzzle it from the tap in my cell.

VI

The day after I entered prison a letter arrived for me from Henry Torrès,* a rather famous lawyer for the Communist Party who also defended revolutionaries from other political tendencies. This lawyer, whose name I'd heard spoken of before, was assisting me at the request of Colomer.

"You should inform the investigating judge that I have taken up your case," the letter from Torrès stated. "If a preliminary hearing is called suddenly, make it known that you are unable to answer any questions unless in my presence."

The letter had arrived in a sealed envelope that I was the first to open. That struck me as odd, but even more interesting was his reference to, "unless in my presence."

I immediately wrote a letter to the judge and another to Torrès, only sealing the envelope for the former.

When Torrès later met me to discuss the case, no prison

---

* Henry Torrès (1891–1966); a lawyer, writer, and politician. Was a member of the French Communist Party in the early 1920s, but defended a number of anarchists in court, including Germaine Berton and Ernesto Bonomini (1903–1986).

Prison Life until Deportation

official was on hand to supervise. We could speak freely and hand over to each other whatever we liked.

A prisoner was thus in a position, provided he had enough money, to create false evidence or destroy actual evidence. A thief could use his stolen money to hire a lawyer and free himself of a criminal charge, or even set about some money-making scheme in prison to cover his legal costs.

*

Every day I lounged about in bed since I was no longer able to buy food or tobacco and had no books to read. It was astonishing to discover just how much I could sleep.

I thought that dozing in the middle of the day might be frowned upon, but I decided to do it anyway until someone scolded me. Unlike the situation in Japanese prisons, the guards rarely visited my cell. One would stop by after I woke in the morning to open the cell door and remove the trash without issuing any signal or command to me. After taking a look around the cell, he would then escort me to the prison yard. Apart from that, no one came around except for the three times when meals were slipped through the slot. We were spared the sort of morning and evening inspections common in Japan. A guard did peek in the cell in the evening upon replacing the afternoon guard, but that was about it.

This left me without any feeling that I was under observation. I was truly living a quiet life on my own with no one to bother me. Apart from sleeping, I did occasionally get out of bed to stroll around the cell.

My Escapes from Japan

On those rounds I kept my thoughts carefree by reading the messages scribbled on the walls. Most messages followed a similar sort of pattern, like:

René de Montmartre
tombé pour vol
1916

The name might be Marcel or Maurice, instead of René, but most hailed from Montmartre, Montparnasse, or some other Parisian den of vice—similar to the Honjo or Asakusa districts in Tokyo. The scribblers also liked to write their nicknames underneath.

dit l'Italien
dit Bonjours aux amis

There were all sorts of nicknames, although I've forgotten most of them. I do recall that one prisoner in for murder went by the name "Iron Arms." Other prisoners were pining for their date of release:

Encore 255 jours à taire
Vive décembre 1923

Another short message that I recall was about hitting an unlucky number:

Ah! 7! Perdu!

Prison Life until Deportation

Alongside it was a drawing of a pair of dice, with the numbers three and four showing.

And then there were passionate messages of the kind you'd never see in Japan.

Riri de Barbes
Fat comme poise
Aime sa femme
Dit Jeane.

Or:

Emile
Adore sa femme
pour la Vie.

And another message, signed "A Bolshevik":

Ce qui mange doit produire
Vive le Soviet

For a bit of fun, I took out my pen and wrote on the wall in thick letters:

E. Ōsugi*

---

* "E." is short for "Ei," the Chinese reading of the kanji character for "Sakae."

My Escapes from Japan

Anarchiste japonais
Arreté S. Denis
Le 1 Mai 1923

*

I was summoned for my preliminary hearing.

The questions started before my lawyer arrived, so I immediately adopted the customary stance of hunching my shoulders and not saying a word. The court quickly ordered a clerk to go find my lawyer.

The proceedings turned out to be quite simple, mainly involving a chat between my lawyer and the judge.

A long list of criminal charges against me had been issued by the Prefecture of Police: Defying a government official by violently resisting a police officer; Disturbing public order; Violating passport regulations; Vagrancy. But the preliminary hearing only investigated the passport violation charge, perhaps because it was the easiest crime to prove.

*

At one point the judge asked me quite politely—although I don't know how he uncovered the information—whether my father was indeed a colonel in the Japanese army. My father was only a major, in fact, but I offered no correction since the judge had made such a point of mentioning it. He seemed to pay me a fair amount of respect, perhaps because the conservative daily *l'Éclair* had published an article by a former socialist familiar with the movement in the Orient who described me as a "renowned scholar."

*

In the initial discussion with my lawyer, the court said that a month or two would be needed prior to the trial to investigate various matters in Lyon. But when my lawyer requested bail at the preliminary hearing it was decided, after considerable deliberation, that the court case would be convened immediately in return for forfeiting the bail request.

My court case was held on May 23, a week after the preliminary hearing. Some fifteen other accused men were waiting with me in the defendants' box, along with a crowd of spectators crammed into the gallery. A bell was sounded and three tottering old judges entered the courtroom, followed by the prosecutor. On the wall behind the judges was a sculpture of the goddess of justice, in white relief.

The court cases began with the head judge saying something in a toothless mumble that even those of us seated nearby struggled to decipher.

"The defendant did this (or that), on this (or that) day. Isn't that correct? All right then . . ." he would say, looking in the direction of the prosecutor. And then, after receiving a nod in return, he would ask if the other two judges had anything to say.

The head judge proceeded to rapidly issue his verdict of so many months in prison and a fine of so many francs, and then summon the next defendant.

I was around the sixth in line, and my case proceeded just like the others.

"You, the defendant, entered France on such-and-such a date, bearing a false passport. Is that correct?"

"Yes."

"Do you have anything else to add?"

"No, I do not."

"So, you acknowledge the truth of the accusations?"

"Yes."

That was the end of the questioning. The prosecutor seemed to have nothing to say and just nodded to the judge.

My lawyer then held forth in his eloquent way for twenty minutes, after which the judge intoned:

"Very well, then. I sentence the defendant to three weeks in prison and a fine of XX francs. Next defendant..."

After the judge pronounced his verdict a constable standing behind us approached and led me away.

In France, all but three days spent in detention prior to a trial count toward the prison sentence. So I had already served my three-week sentence by the time of the trial and could be released the following day.

The news came as a crushing disappointment.

*

Four or five defendants were kept in the detention cell of the courthouse prior to the hearings. During the wait, they were grousing noisily about their own cases. Each recounted whatever crime he had committed and speculated on what might be said in court to get off with a lighter sentence. In response, another might disagree, pointing to how saying such a thing would only backfire in this or that way. And yet another might say, "There's nothing to worry about: you'll only get three or four months, tops." The talk was the same sort of chatter often heard in a detention cell outside a Japanese courthouse, mostly about money: how someone managed to get hold of a few hundred or a few thousand francs through this or that scam; utterly boring banter.

I didn't say a word, using the time instead to inspect the graffiti on the walls.

A bas l'avocat official!

That line showed up in a couple places. Then there were the sort of messages I'd seen in my own prison cell. I found several professions of love written by a man who worshiped a lady in Brittany, along with some rather good drawings of her. I even came across a few odd erotic sketches.

As I was carefully reading each message, I felt a tap on my shoulder.

"Hey there. What are you in for? *Robbery?*"

It was our resident expert on criminal convictions who had been holding forth with predictions on how many months his associates would be in for.

"Ah, well, something like that," I responded coolly.

"Is that so? What did you steal? Are you from Indo-China?"

"No, I'm Japanese," I said, thinking it less trouble to tell him the truth if he was so keen to ask questions.

"A *Japanese* thief? Don't run into many of those. When did you arrive in France?"

The expert kept at his questioning, which I tried to cut short by being even more honest:

"Just after I got here the cops got me for making a speech on May Day."

"Oh, so you're in for a political crime," he said abruptly and then turned to recommence discussion with his esteemed colleagues.

It was at that moment that another man, who had been among the others but only listening to them, came over to where I was. The man, around forty and with one hand that seemed a bit odd, began by saying:

"They nabbed me, too, at the May Day demonstration at place du Combat. Where were you arrested?"

The man looked like a worker; dressed in shabby clothes but quite well spoken. Place du Combat was a public space near CGTU headquarters. Many anarchists associated with *le Libertaire* had probably gathered there. I seemed to have found someone of a like mind, so I tried to find out more from him.

"They picked me up in Saint Denis," I said. "What was it like at Combat?"

"There was quite a crowd. The ones I was with didn't care much for the speeches, so we led a group that dashed off and smashed up a few cars and held up traffic."

It turned out that he was an anarchist; a former factory worker who had injured his hand in the war. He did odd jobs

Prison Life until Deportation

to scrape together a living. The man told me that the year before there had been a riot at Combat, but that he and everyone else had escaped arrest. But this year the police cracked down. Even though the disturbance was no different from before, around a hundred protesters were arrested.

"The police played rough this time around, and my lawyer says the courts will come down hard on us too. I suppose you'll just be deported, but I'm looking at six months behind bars."

While I was talking to him, the time had come for us to be taken to the courtroom. When I returned to the holding cell later, the same man was there.

"Well, we're both getting out of here," he said. "I was handed a six-month sentence, as expected, but thanks to 'His Honor' and my lawyer's persistence that was changed to a two-year suspended sentence."

He looked pleased but let out a sarcastic laugh as he shook my hand. After a while, we all were taken out of the detention cell and transported to the prison.

VII

The next morning, May 24, the police took us to the detention cell at the courthouse. They said they were going to place us in the Grand Salon, which turned out to be next to the other detention cell where we had been held before, with the same heavy iron door. And it was indeed grand: spacious enough to accommodate a lecture for five or even six hundred people.

The courthouse and adjacent police ministry had once been royal palaces, apparently, and this room was some great hall from that era. The floor was cement, but there were several large marble pillars supporting a magnificent ceiling. Entering the room, I saw a few groups of half a dozen men discussing one thing or another. I wandered toward one group of younger, more respectable-looking men.

They were speaking in French but something about their accent gave me the impression they were foreigners; their faces did not look very French. A tall, Italian-looking man among them glanced at me and asked right away:

"They're deporting you as well, eh?"

When I said yes, he added:

"Ah, it looks like it. All of us, in fact. Care for a smoke?" he asked, holding out a cigarette case.

We talked about all sorts of things, but nothing gave me the impression that these men had done anything particularly bad. Since they had landed in this prison and were now to be deported, I figured they must have been caught on some passport or *carte d'identité* violation. And judging from their ladykiller looks and demeanors, some of them must have made money pimping as a *maquereau*.

None of the men had the least intention of returning home to Italy, Spain, Portugal, or wherever they were from; nor did any of them plan to head off to some other country. No, they were all bent on returning to France—and to Paris, in particular.

"But if you're deported, won't you have to leave France," I asked, finding their nonchalance a bit odd.

Prison Life until Deportation

"Not many of those ordered to leave actually do. We're going to be called up and issued a deportation order. And that's the end of the matter as far as the authorities are concerned. Where we go is our own business."

This man seemed to find my own incredulity rather incredible. For two of the men, it was their second time to be issued a deportation order.

In my mind, "deportation" was a situation where a time limit is set to leave and in the meantime the police keep a close eye on you, as had happened to my Russian friend Kozlov in Japan. But it was nothing like that in France. It was reassuring to know that we were simply given a sheet of paper with the deportation order and then told to get out; and that nothing would happen to anyone (even a repeat offender) who simply ignored the order.

Finally they started to call out our names. One prisoner after another was summoned to be told which jail he would be sent to, until I was the only one left.

When my turn finally came, instead of being taken upstairs as the others had, I was led to the same small room near the entrance where my possessions had been examined at the time I first entered prison. My foreign friends of a moment ago already had their possessions and were on the way out.

"So, did they sort you out upstairs?" the handsome Italian prisoner asked me.

"No, not yet."

"That must mean that you're not being deported and are free to go right away," the man said as he was leaving.

That did not seem to be the case, though, and I was feeling

more and more anxious to be the only one left.

*

I was handed my things but not released. Soon after, another guard came to take me to police headquarters. There, my time was taken up, among other things, with the same physical examination I had undergone before, until finally, around midday. I was taken to the office of the deputy secretary, who handed me the order for immediate deportation issued by the interior minister. And it was *immediate*. I was ordered to leave right away, accompanied by my police shadow.

"You must leave France at once, but we can't allow you to exit the city to the east. You'll have to go west, via Spain. How does that suit you?"

It wasn't really a matter of what suited me. I would just have to go wherever I must. But Spain was fine with me; it was a country I had always wanted to visit.

"I don't mind," I said, "but of course I'll need permission from the Japanese authorities to travel there. What should I do?"

"Just wait over there; we'll negotiate with the Japanese embassy for you," was the response. And later I was led to the Police des Étrangers office, with which I was already quite familiar.

*

At the office, I saw almost a hundred plainclothes detectives

Prison Life until Deportation

at their desks, sifting through similar looking documents that they were pulling out of or putting back into files. On each file a name was written, no doubt all considered dangerous individuals whom the police must keep a close eye on, and inside seemed to be a dozen or more sheets of paper.

The detectives, seated in the middle of the room, occasionally cast me a quick glance as they flipped through the pages of their files. Like their counterparts in Japan, not a single one had a look of humanity in his eyes. Their expressions reminded me of the thieves and swindlers I had seen in La Santé Prison—or even worse.

It was around noon. All of them were about to head off for their midday meal. I asked the man next to me about my own lunch, and he went to check with someone nearby who seemed to be in charge. I was told that they'd get me anything I wanted, so I listed up some extravagant items and also asked for a bottle of good white wine.

There were always four or five of the detectives on hand, and around two o'clock those who had gone out to lunch began to trickle back to the office.

The person sent to the Japanese embassy on my behalf had yet to return. I asked several times for permission to go to the deputy secretary's office but it was not granted.

Tired of waiting and bored—and annoyed by all the looks I was getting from the detectives—I kept taking sips from my bottle of wine, even though I'm not much of a drinker.

Finally, around four in the afternoon, someone arrived from the deputy secretary's office to escort me there. I met the deputy secretary and talked to him for a while until a tall

Japanese man arrived who had a long and rather hazy visage. He was accompanied by the policeman who had been sent to fetch him from the embassy. I had heard the Japanese man's name mentioned before: it was Sugimura Tarō, the first secretary at the Japanese embassy in Paris.

After exchanging greetings with the deputy secretary, Sugimura asked for permission to discuss something with me in private. The deputy secretary opened a door to a separate room for us to use.

"I just learned of your deportation order from the policeman sent to the embassy" Sugimura began. "I came here to do whatever I can to negotiate on your behalf."

He then went into some detail of how he could mediate. The Japanese government had forbidden the embassy from issuing any passport to me. This meant I could not receive permission to travel to Spain. The embassy would ask for the deportation to be delayed several months and pledge to take responsibility for me in the meantime.

After our talk, Sugimura made this request to the deputy secretary using extremely polite language, but was told that a deportation order, once issued, cannot be rescinded. Hearing this, Sugimura said that he would have to return to the embassy to consult further with the other officials there.

*

I asked the deputy secretary whether the Spanish officials would allow me to cross the border from France if the embassy didn't issue me a passport."

"I don't know. That's up to them."

"And what would I do if Spain won't let me in?"

"All I can say is that if you are found in France, you'll be put right back in prison."

His response reminded me of an interesting story my French teacher once had told me back in the days when I was enrolled at a language school. It was a tale of a thief who was about to be arrested near a border and tried to escape by crossing over into the neighboring country. Once he stepped over the border he stuck out his tongue like a child at the policeman giving chase, who stamped his fists on the ground in frustration.

With that story in mind, I jokingly said:

"So, in that case, I'll either be thrown in a Spanish prison or one in France; or perhaps each side will grab one leg and leave me suspended for days in the middle?"

"I suppose that is the situation," he replied quite earnestly.

*

I was sent back to the first room and waited a couple of hours there before being summoned again to the deputy secretary's office, where I was told—perhaps because of Sugimura's intervention—that I was to depart immediately for Marseille.

"You aren't allowed to meet anyone. An officer will escort you to the station and you will have to board the first available train."

My Escapes from Japan

*

We arrived at Gare du Lyon by automobile, not long before the departure of the eight o'clock express train.

I saw a police officer who was waiting until my train pulled out of the station and then seemed to turn around to leave. I had been told that my departure and arrival time had been wired to the Marseille police, so I thought it would cause the comrades in Lyon too much trouble if I stopped off there along the way. But I arrived in Marseille the next morning to find no police—uniformed or otherwise—waiting for me at the station.

I went to the Japanese consulate after I found a place to stay. There I met a newly appointed consul named Suga, who just a week before had been working under Sugimura at the embassy.

Suga went to the police station in Marseille, where he succeeded in insisting that the "first boat," which I had been ordered to take, would be a Japanese vessel. He then went to the ticket office for the ship and negotiated so that I could purchase a berth without a passport. It was arranged for me to travel on the Hakone Maru, a Japanese vessel scheduled to depart in exactly one week.

While awaiting the departure, I telegraphed home and also sent telegraphs and letters to friends in Paris and Lyon. What set my mind at ease as I made my preparations was that none of my friends or comrades had experienced too much trouble

Prison Life until Deportation

on my account.*

*

Since Paris had issued me an "immediate deportation" notice, I expected to be closely watched in Marseille. Hoping to limit that intrusion as much as possible, I stayed at the nicest hotel in the city.

For the first few days I was on the lookout for police surveillance, but I could not detect anything; nor did the hotel treat me differently from other guests. I could stroll around freely outside without anyone tailing me. And when I returned to the hotel, no questions were asked about where I had gone.

The consulate apparently asked the police casually about me, but they did not send anyone to meet me at the train station when I arrived in Marseille. On my train there had been a robbery, which seemed to cause the police some problems, but I don't think that can account for why no one was sent to the station to meet my train. I imagined that it would be necessary to present myself at police headquarters immediately upon arrival, but the consulate informed me that it wasn't necessary since they had gone there to sort things out for me.

The situation called to mind the talk among the lady killers back at the Grand Salon; my deportation order, supposedly so strict, had turned out to be as lax as those for my fellow

---

* He never learned that his Chinese comrade, Shō Keishū (see footnote on p. 76), was deported from France for his connection to Ōsugi.

prisoners. It reminded me of the Hungarian comrade I'd seen at the Libertaire office. He was later deported, but just a few days after that I saw him strolling around the neighborhood again. My lawyer, too, following my trial, gave me a casual, "See you later" as he departed.

If this was standard procedure, there was no reason to take the term "immediate" too literally and leave right away; or even if you did leave, you could always return again. In my inexperience I had thought that once the order had been issued, you must leave; and it was with that expectation fully in mind that I had taken the stage to give my speech on May Day.

I considered fleeing Marseille to travel around illegally, provided I could round up some money from Paris or somewhere else. I thought about bouncing around here and there, maybe heading back to Paris or traveling to Germany or Italy, or wherever else I wanted to go.

I spent a night engrossed in these plans, not that it would have been that difficult to arrange. I had pondered the idea before and come up with various schemes. All I needed was the money and I could be off.

Nearly resolved to attempt an escape, I made little excursions of a half or an entire day to see whether anyone was keeping an eye on me, and thereby confirmed that I was not under surveillance. I discussed the plan at the home of a comrade in Marseille, who told me that the necessary means were at hand.

Regretfully, I had to abandon my plan of escape when a letter mailed from Japan prior to my arrest arrived; it listed all the problems back home and asked why I hadn't returned yet.

Prison Life until Deportation

It was enough to convince me that I had better behave myself and go home.

*

Two days before my departure the consulate sent me a second-class ticket to Yokohama along with a bill:

> Bill due: 5,000 francs
> Date
> Ōsugi Sakae
> Consul, Mr. Suga

On the following day some money from Japan also arrived. It was enough to purchase a third-class ticket, but I used it to hastily buy some gifts before my departure.

When it came time to board the ship, I first offered my farewells to the police, as recommended by the consulate. I went to the police station in the evening, carrying my hand luggage; a friend was to bring the rest of my baggage before the ship departed the next morning. After visiting the police station I intended to board the ship for a moment to confirm where I would be sleeping and then go back on land to attend a farewell party with friends.

The head of police had a long telegraph in front of him from Paris headquarters. After looking through various things, he assigned a detective to escort me to the ship.

On board, I took care of a few things and was ready to leave to meet my friends for dinner. But just as I was about to step off the ship, the detective ran up the gangplank with three others to block my way.

"Once you've boarded you can't leave. You've already crossed the border. If you step off the ship you are reentering France and will be locked up for six months."

It was absurd. I protested that he should have told me that before I boarded the ship, but to no avail.

I had a crew member telephone my friends to let them know what had happened and then went into my cabin to sleep.

*

The ship lifted anchor early on the morning of June 3.

Tokyo – August 10, 1923

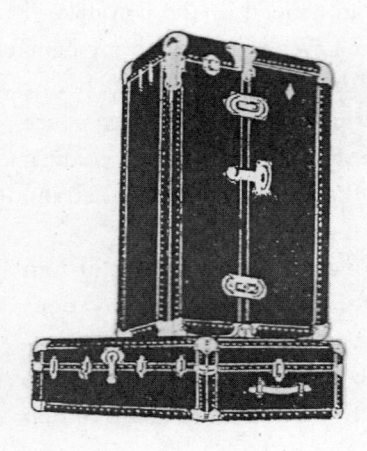

Assorted Stories from My Trip Overseas

I

On my journeys I tend to travel to my destination in grand style but return home a pauper. My recent trip to France was an exception, however, and indeed the exact opposite. I returned from France in comfort, traveling on the second-class ticket the consulate purchased for me. If things had worked out better, I might even have traveled first class. That was the embassy's original plan, but quite a few of the Japanese officials in Paris shared the strong opinion that I deserved nothing better than a third-class ticket. The difference was split in the end; hence my second-class berth.

On my way to Europe I had, for once, traveled within my means, on a third-class ticket. The third-class cabins on the French ocean liner were like those on the special third-class deck of a mail liner, with rooms for two or four people. I stayed in a two-person cabin with a young Chinese student.

With me in third class were around eight Chinese students, both men and women. We shared a table for our meals. Everyone spoke a bit of English and a couple of them spoke Japanese. But, for whatever reason, I didn't get on very well with these students, preferring to spend my time with passengers on the fourth-class deck.

Traveling in fourth class were twenty or thirty Chinese workers who had boarded at Shanghai, around a dozen French sailors, and fifteen or so Russians. I immediately forged a friendship with a French sailor and many of the young Russian students. The sailor had served on a gunboat on the Yangtze River and was returning to France now that his enlistment was up. Unlike the other sailors, who would stroll around on deck together while humming a song, he was always off by himself in a corner reading some book. The sailor, still quite young, had an intelligent look about him.

I was eager to make his acquaintance right away. As practice for my French, I greeted him with a *Bonjour, monsieur*.

After we had asked about each other's background and destination, the conversation quickly turned to the labor movement in France. This was because I had claimed to be a twenty-eight-year-old student of sociology who was traveling to France to study the labor issue.

The French sailor was not a participant in the movement himself, nor had he done much research on the subject, so there wasn't a lot to learn from our conversation in that respect. But his bitter attack on military service and war was quite interesting in view of his social background.

"After just six months or a year of the Great War in Europe," he said, "what a shambles France became." xxxxxxxxx
xxxxxxxxxxxxxxxxxxxxxxxxxxxxxxxxxxxxxxxxxxxxxxxxxx
xxxxxxxxxxxxxxxxxxxxxxxxxxxxxxxxxxxxxxxxxxxxxxxxxx
xxxxxxxxxxxxxxxxxxxxxxxxxxxxxxxxxxxxxxxxxxxxxxxxxx
xxxxxxxxxxxxxxxxxxxxxxxxxxxxxxxxxxxxxxxxxxxxxxxxxx
xxxxxxxxxxxxxxx

II

xxxxxxxxxxxxxxxxxxxxxxxxxxxxxxxxx In talking to the sailor and to other people later in France, I was surprised to learn just how widespread and vehement anti-war sentiment was.

Many had been killed for holding such views. Others were thrown in prison, where many still remained. And quite a few had fled and were still living an underground existence.

Before my arrival in France, and during my stay, there were demands for amnesty to be granted to those labeled "criminals" for opposing the war and to those who had fallen victim to the reactionary postwar political wave. This plea featured prominently as the first demand voiced at the May Day meetings. On several occasions the French government had pledged to meet the demand, but it remained a mere promise.

A few days before I left France, the leader of the *Mutins de la mer noire*, apparently a Communist Party member who was still in prison, was put up as a candidate to replace a lower-house parliamentary deputy representing a Paris suburb. The candidate won the uncontested election in an unprecedented landslide.* The other parties had intended to run a joint candidate to oppose him but dropped the idea when they saw the tremendous support he enjoyed.

The election was also interesting for the fact that more people abstained than voted. Since the Parisian suburbs are mainly working-class areas, the election results revealed that half of the workers (at least among those living in the suburbs) backed the mutineer, while the other half cared little for politics.

Around the same time, the mutiny leader was also elected to the municipal council of the same suburb. As for what happened later—whether he became a parliamentary deputy or council member as the workers had hoped, or the government instead managed to have the election declared invalid and keep him in prison—I never found out.

Although my sailor friend Jean criticized military service, opposed war, and exulted in the mutinies, he was certainly *not* a communist, nor did he adhere to any other "dangerous" ideology.

I teased him a bit by saying, "You sound like some sort of socialist"; and he proudly affirmed that, indeed, he was. But when I asked him what he meant by that, I gathered from his explanation that he would be satisfied if capitalists and work-

---

* André Marty (1886–1956); a French naval officer involved in the mutinies aboard the battleships *Jean Bart* and *France* in the Black Sea in opposition to the navy's support of the Russian White Army. Was "political commissar" of the International Brigades during the Spanish Civil War.

ers could somehow "share the profits."

Most of the Europeans who call themselves socialists hold that sort of view. I once described the leading German Social Democrat Bebel, and his ilk, as nothing more than Ōkuma Shigenobu* with a few more hairs on his head. But today the stock of socialists has fallen even lower, and that of the communists continues to fall.

When Jean had some time on his hands, he liked to take out a cheap copy of Shakespeare's collected works and carefully read from it, line by line. Or he would pore over a thick stack of letters and postcards, with a grin on his face. The letters were from his bride-to-be, the daughter of peasants in his native Brittany. He was counting the days until they could be reunited and live a quiet country life together.

III

By talking to Jean a number of times I made the acquaintance of the young Russians he had befriended, all of whom could speak a bit of English.

Most of the Russians were young, in their early or middle twenties, and all had boarded from the Chinese city Harbin. The older among them had left the Russian army after first fighting against the Germans and Austrians, and later against the Bolshevik Red Army. This had taken them from

---

* Ōkuma Shigenobu (1838–1922); Japan's prime minister from 1914 to 1916. Received a Western education as a young man.

Europe to Russia, then to Siberia, from where they traveled to Harbin. Now they were headed to Germany or France to continue their studies.

I became the best of friends with this group of Russians and soon was calling them by their nicknames—like "Pechka" for Pyotr or "Mika" for Mikhail. And they called me "Masa-chika" (because Masaichi was the assumed name I was using).

They were lively and cheerful, always talking, drinking tea, singing, pulling pranks, and dancing. The Russians were the only ones on the ship behaving in that way.

They let me join in their antics, but what interested me most about them was the chance to hear the tales Pechka, Mika, and others told of the Russian civil war. I was especially interested to learn that they joined the counter-revolutionary forces in Europe or Siberia even though they weren't interested in restoring the monarchy and did not ideologically oppose the revolution.

It was their hatred for the Bolsheviks, I learned, that led them to join the counter-revolutionary army. The atrocities committed by the government against the peasants had driven these men to take up arms against it.

The Bolsheviks, backed by force, had ordered the peasants to hand over food supplies. When this demand was shunned, the "worker-peasant government" quickly dispatched troops to punish the defiance. Entire villages were torched, the men slaughtered, even women and children flogged; the troops took every last speck of flour and the seeds needed for the next planting season. The peasants who escaped into the mountains and forests became "bandits," ruthless partisans determined to avenge those atrocities.

My Russian friends fought alongside these desperate peasants. Like them, they were hardly counter-revolutionaries bent on restoring the monarchy. Rather, they'd joined up with the White Army because they saw it as the only force through which they could protect themselves and seek vengeance from the Bolsheviks.

Once in France I learned more about how the White Army had allied with peasant partisans here and there to combat the Bolsheviks, while also fighting against the anti-Bolshevik partisans who had seen through the counter-revolutionary ambitions of the Whites. And then there were the many peasants swallowed up, along with their meager possessions, into the Red Army as conscripts.

It was a chaotic struggle in which something like a million Russian peasants lost their lives. This supposed revolutionary struggle was in fact a civil war in which revenge and counter-revenge piled up; a ruthless fight to the death that is hair-raising to even contemplate.

IV

Along with the young Russians, there were seven or eight men a bit older who were Poles, Russians, Czechs, and Jews. Those with wives and children had placed them in the third-class cabin, while traveling in fourth class themselves with the other men.

These older men included a Russian, around sixty years old,

who was traveling fourth class with his twenty-year-old son while his wife was in a third-class cabin. This older Russian was every inch the peasant, not refined in the least. His thick salt-and-pepper moustache seemed to stretch out a foot on each side, lending him a stern look. On the breast of his tattered suit were over half a dozen small military decorations. His old wife had the same sort of dirty, unsophisticated face, while the son looked feebleminded, his mouth always half open.

The three were always sprawled out on the wicker chairs on the third-class deck, but one day the old man came over to where I was and greeted me in Japanese with a *kon'nichi wa*, and then began jabbering in Russian. He was pointing to the medals on his chest. Listening more closely, I could make out that he seemed to be saying, *Ya geroy, ya geroy*. I knew that *ya* meant "I" and *geroy* was "hero." Having no choice but to agree with him, I replied, *Da, da, ty geroy*. He was saying something about how he had been a general during the war with Japan. I suppose that was when he received the medals that he was pointing to.

Later I asked Pechka about the man. It turned out that he was indeed a war hero who had risen in the ranks to become a general and was unmatched for his bravery. But Pechka and his friends had little time for this war hero.

And just as they shunned this old man, the young Russians looked down on Jews in the most appalling way.

One day, I recall, a young Polish pianist was irate at the Chinese workers on board for some reason; he cursed that they were not even human and good for nothing. Hearing

Assorted Stories from My Trip Overseas

this, Pechka and his friends went over to the pianist and tore into him, insisting that Chinese were human beings too, no different from Russians or Poles. The argument dragged on for much of the day, until both sides were red in the face.

Yet Pechka and these same friends utterly shunned the Jews on board the ship. When I happened to talk to some of the Jewish passengers, the Russians shot me dirty looks for the rest of the day.

There was also a high-born Russian woman[*] I met on the ship through Pechka's group. The woman had once been a history student at Moscow University and later studied in Paris. She was quite progressive and free-thinking. Whenever our ship docked at a port, we would disembark together and drive out far into the countryside to enjoy seeing how the people lived on the land. The woman had a great fondness for the customs of rural life she witnessed.

Yet once, when we disembarked at Ville de Djibouti in the evening and found all the shops closed except one owned by a Jew, this same woman returned to the ship without buying the ostrich feather and other items she had been so keen to purchase. She had stepped into the shop, saying they probably would not have what she was looking for, and the moment she saw the slightly pointed nose of the man who seemed to be the shop owner she turned pale and rushed out. I felt dumbfounded as she grabbed my hand to beat that hasty retreat, trembling, it seemed. She had no intention to spend another instant in what was to her such a distasteful place.

---

[*] "Madame N."

V

At Haiphong and Saigon, two ports of the French colony Cochinchina, our ship was boarded by a horde of French soldiers and sailors whose enlistment periods were up—mostly drunkards and wastrels. Unlike the young French sailors I had met earlier, who still had their humanity intact (even if overly disciplined and a bit dim), these new arrivals, mostly in their mid-thirties, seemed more like livestock than men to me, grunting like pigs or wild animals.

One of these military men, apparently the most popular among them, came tottering over to me one day to mumble a few words.

"Yep, here's all to know about me," he said, holding out his *Carnet du soldat* impressively listing where he had served as a bugler or private first class, mostly in the colonies—two years here and three years there, and so on, over an eighteen-year career. Nothing was listed under the heading "Disciplinary problems." But under "Commendations" there was quite a lot. He had been discharged from the military due to illness, apparently.

"And now I got this money," he said, brandishing four or five ten-franc bills from a tattered wallet, and then let out a laugh that made it hard to know whether he found the situation unfair or was instead happy about it.

These drunken soldiers were not so bad, but the enlisted men traveling in third class were simply insufferable. These

Assorted Stories from My Trip Overseas

were the ones who acted like wild animals, the spitting images of bears and wild boars. And their wives were just as hopeless.

Looking at their faces made me think that it must have been bastards like these who committed the murder I read about in a newspaper article that same day while on shore.

A French-language paper put out by the local Indochinese had covered the story, which was featured under a large headline. It was a simple case where a local merchant had been drowned in a river. But it was more than that because such incidents occurred regularly. They were never solved; or perhaps I should say the culprits could not be publically named. The case I read about was surrounded by such suspicious circumstances.

My French friend Jean shared my intuition about the case. "Lord knows what they are up to. For the sake of a pension and the chance to live like scoundrels they travel all the way out to these colonies for an enlistment of ten or fifteen years. Soldiering is a way of life for them."

Whenever I ran into these soldiers behaving outrageously on deck or in the dining hall, they never once gave me a word of greeting.

Later, after I arrived in France, I saw large army notices posted on walls here and there calling for recruits to the colonies, with figures in bold print explaining how salaries and pensions rise depending on whether the enlistment was three, five, ten, or fifteen years.

My Escapes from Japan

VI

I think it was around Hong Kong that the ship was boarded by a dignified elderly man who seemed to be from Annam,* with a white moustache and thin long beard.

I wanted to have a word with him but did not have the chance before he disembarked at Sai Kung. A young student from Annam who boarded at Haiphong told me that the elderly man was a member of the royal family and now held an honorary position as the minister of the army or some such title. The sight of a former Russian general strutting around on the third-class deck had seemed comical, but seeing this other man there too struck me as tragic, somehow.

Yet the elderly man maintained his bonhomie and an inviolable dignity. In contrast, the average person from Annam was not a very pleasant sight: hopelessly petty-minded and lacking in pride. What made it even more unpleasant for me was that the Annam people more closely resembled the Japanese in appearance and mannerisms than any other nation in East Asia.

Walking around Haiphong and Sai Kung, I saw how the people in Annam had been reduced to a beggar's existence. If you stepped into a shop, the only ones enjoying a somewhat human life were Chinese or Indian. Meanwhile, the French

---

* A French protectorate corresponding to the southern and central region of present-day Vietnam.

were living like kings.

At Sai Kung I traveled with my Russian friend Madame N. out into the countryside, where we saw an elementary school alongside the road. There were two barrack-like buildings, open on all sides, with around thirty students who were being taught in each. When we entered the school, all of the students stood up and bowed to us, and the teacher quickly stepped down from the platform at the front of the classroom to greet us in a rather overly polite way. That alone left a bad impression on me.

In response to a question by Madame N., the teacher, with great pride, informed us that the students are not taught any Chinese characters; instead, a type of Roman alphabet is used to teach them the Annam language. This in itself is of course not a bad thing, and in fact much to the good, but I couldn't accept how it had been done at the behest of the French colonial government; nor did I like how the teacher took such pride in the fact.

The Annam children, receiving this sort of education, gradually learn French, and the most promising students are sent to study in France. After returning to their native land, they either become school teachers or petty government officials. The young Annam student I spoke of earlier was one of the students sent to France to study. He had worked for the government upon returning, and was now going back to France again to resume his studies.

In China, I'd seen how the Chinese who served foreigners had adopted their snobbish attitude. The young Annam man was not like that, but there were such types here and there.

This was particularly true of the soldiers and policemen, who behaved atrociously.

Being sent over to study in France had a particular significance in some cases, however. You see, not all the Annam people were so small-minded and humble; there was a variety of types. And the French officials had to allow them a certain freedom of speech. But whenever a person emerged who had some firmness of principles and popularity among the people, he was immediately sent to study in Paris, given a monthly stipend to live on, and shut up in some hotel like a prisoner.

I had intended to meet one such student in Paris, but various things got in the way to prevent our meeting.

VII

The inhabitants of British or Dutch colonies like Malay, Java, and Sumatra were also as destitute as those living in Annam. Any halfway decent shop in Singapore was run by Chinese or Indians, whereas the locals were all peasants or coolies. Those Chinese and Indian merchants behaved like thieves, but their compatriots working in the street as laborers looked every bit as pitiful as the locals. My heart was drawn to the Indians in particular, who, despite their pitch-black eyes that looked somewhat menacing, in fact had very meek expressions when you drew near to them. These Chinese, Indian, and local coolies were treated like dogs or horses, their emaciated bodies struck with sticks or kicked while they were working.

On my return voyage to Japan, a passenger who boarded at

Assorted Stories from My Trip Overseas

Sumatra told me that terrible acts of revenge occasionally are carried out by the natives against their masters. They might shoot poison darts produced secretly in their hamlets or fire a bullet at a car from out of the dense jungle of palm and rubber trees. Injuries from such assaults were as common as those from a tiger or rhinoceros attack.

And it was not all acts of personal revenge. Already the local workers in Sumatra were aware of themselves as wage laborers and had formed a large labor union. Just before our ship landed there the railway workers union called a general strike that lasted for a month, from May to June.

In response, the Dutch officials quickly amended the laws to require permission a week prior to any assembly, effectively making it impossible for workers to gather. And the main leaders of the union were rounded up and thrown into prison. The strike was only finally put down when the army was mobilized to back up the police.

These local workers were organized not only according to their jobs but in line with their religious beliefs, and at times religion was the thing around which they were most firmly united. Along with their desire to free themselves from wage slavery was a yearning for national or religious autonomy, which heightened their fervor.

From local newspapers I learned that, although there is not yet much influence from "Bolshevik propaganda," socialist thought in the broad sense has very much taken root. If the Indian or Chinese workers of the same religious faith were united under socialism it would create problems for the English and Dutch colonies.

When I was looking out on the port of Hong Kong, I heard the Chinese students issuing indignant patriotic oaths. And they engaged in high-flown talk about what would happen if France did not return Annam. I had also seen how they remained in their cabins, angrily refusing to eat, in protest against the treatment of a supposed Chinese thief who had been beaten to a pulp by French soldiers after he stowed away on the ship. But these same students pounced upon a fellow Chinese, a coolie rickshaw driver, with punches and kicks over some trifling question of money. When I saw this, I lost all sympathy for them. Thankfully, though, these patriots never bothered me.

VIII

It was somewhere near Columbo, I think, that I learned by telegraph that France had occupied the Ruhr, and that the Communist Party leader Cachin and others had been arrested.

The situations for Germany and France before and after the war were nearly reversed, at least militarily, now that the German army had been effectively destroyed. France, instead of restoring its own productive power, was concentrating most of its energy on stepping up military preparations. Germany was not about to respond to this provocation, being no match for France. But it did seem possible that France, which was becoming a nexus of militarism and reaction, would be swept along by the momentum toward some reckless act. I entered France with this strong premonition that something might arise from the situation.

I arrived to find, however, that Marseille, Lyon, and Paris were quite placid. The atmosphere gave me little sense that another war was looming—or at least I saw no sign of that from the life of the common people, who looked carefree, as if there were no problems at all.

Among the people I had expected to find the embers of the fervent wartime nationalism that was still being fanned, but saw no trace anywhere, apart from the sputtering of three or four royalist newspapers, most notably *l'Action française*.

Even in Lyon, the most conservative and religious of French cities—and in a suburban district known for its churches, no less—I didn't see a single copy of *l'Action française* in the half-dozen kiosks I came across. Whenever I asked one of the old ladies working behind the counter about the royalist newspapers, I was told that they had sold well during the war but weren't worth stocking now for lack of interest.

In walking around the cities I was sure to encounter a handful of men—or more likely a dozen—who were missing an arm or had a prosthetic leg; all victims of the war, needless to say. With such sights always in view, I thought there was no chance for another war to break out now.

Instead of taking advantage of this mood, the communists and the CGT, in their meetings and articles opposing war and the occupation of the Ruhr, offered nothing more than rhetoric and bluster. Even the occasional demonstrations did not lead anywhere. Far from stopping the occupation, such actions could not even lessen its severity.

Among the French troops as well there was no opposition in the barracks to the extension by a month or two of their two-year enlistment period, which began in 1921 and was supposed to have ended in March. Soldiers had little idea where they would be dispatched next, either. The Communist Party's newspaper, *l'Humanité*, ran articles every day about these issues, but it didn't seem to create any great stir. The communists made a point of warning people not to provoke the authorities and for everyone to protest in a civilized manner.

On Sundays, I saw soldiers walking up and down the boulevards, kissing their girlfriends while resting a hand on their broad hips.

All looked peaceful in the world.

IX

One of my main occupations since arriving in France was to read nearly every French newspaper in the morning.

Soon after my arrival I learned from *l'Humanité* about the coal-mine strike in the north of France. Every day the strike was growing in strength, until some seventy or eighty thousand miners had joined in. Yet the capitalist newspapers only dedicated a few lines to the strike each day. The papers claimed that more and more miners were returning to work, and that the strike involved just a few hundred or at most a thousand workers.

Later, when eight thousand *midinettes* seamstresses went

Assorted Stories from My Trip Overseas

out on strike, you would never have known from reading the capitalist papers. Hundreds of women's organizations were invited to the factories for demonstrations, clashing with the police everywhere, but only a few lines appeared in those papers; most articles claimed that the strike had ended. Although the newspapers asserted a number of times that the women had returned to their factories, they were in fact raising a clamor at strike headquarters in the CGTU building, thousands laughing merrily and singing.

The workers described this newspaper bias as "sabotage" against their movement, and it was indeed how journalists treated every manifestation of the workers' movement.

There is nothing odd about this; it's perfectly natural. What's strange is the response of capitalist papers in Japan, which scream and shout every time there is a strike or something of the sort.

What surprised me in France was that there were workers and workers' organizations that were sabotaging the strike. I'm speaking of the CGT, which was once full of revolutionary bluster. Around the time of the coal miners' strike, CGT leaders were mollifying the workers with talk of how the nation's enemies were trying to stifle the coal industry at a moment of crisis between France and Germany.

Soon after I returned home from France, I heard that the Yūaikai union in Japan had followed a similar approach to put down a strike of automobile workers. It made me realize how the same types of despicable tactics are used everywhere.

The Socialist Party and the CGT tried to sabotage whatever the Communist Party and the CGTU were doing, just as the communists themselves sabotaged the activities of the anarchists.

After I was arrested on May Day, *l'Humanite* dedicated a full column to the incident. But the next day they discovered I was an anarchist and never wrote a single word about my subsequent trial and deportation. Meanwhile the royalist newspaper *l'Action francaise*, no matter what the incident, makes a point of inserting something about an "anarchist inciting murder."

This is the sort of cheap, negative sabotage that exists alongside the more positive sabotage of obstructing production.

In a recent issue of *Tokyo asahi shimbun*, its Paris correspondent described Germaine Berton as a "young female political fanatic." This was not that negative compared with the descriptions of her in the French capitalist newspapers, where she was called a "prostitute," a "traitor in the pay of the Germans," or even a "police dog."

The newspaper of l'Union anarchiste, *le Libertaire*, was suppressed almost every week for running articles defending Berton, and its editors and subscribers were thrown into La Santé Prison.

X

On the evening of my arrival in Paris, I left my lodgings to walk around after eating dinner. It was surprising to see that the district where I was staying closely resembled Asakusa in

Assorted Stories from My Trip Overseas

Tokyo, albeit an even nastier version.

It was a slum and red-light district; a center of raucous theatrical shows. The area was full of dirty restaurants, cafés, and hotels. On the streets were tiny exhibition areas for shows, billiard halls, and shooting galleries. And this stretched on for blocks and blocks.

Beneath a signboard for a show, featuring dark-skinned savages waging war against each other, were half-naked boys and girls painted pitch-black who were brandishing bows and arrows as they screamed and shouted. Next to them was a huge painted sign for the "Human Spider," an arachnid with the face of a man. A pool hall was nearby, adjacent to a roulette game, then a shooting gallery, a contest of bobbing for bottles, and every other sort of stand imaginable. What was nowhere to be seen was a shop selling any sort of ordinary wares.

I saw a merry-go-round with toy cars, benches, horses, and lions on a large platform that spun around to the sound of loud, brassy music. Some adults, rather advanced in age, were on the ride enjoying themselves. Below that area was a swing shaped like a small boat; it was filled with young men and women and swayed back and forth, on the verge of tipping over. A huge spinning wheel was another attraction; the riders, seated in crates hanging from the side, screamed with joy as the wheel rotated around and baskets next to each other collided. Street photographers were interspersed among the crowd, asking people to pose for a snapshot.

And alongside the groups of carnies that were running these attractions were the vehicles in which they made their homes and used to travel all over France and from country to country, about the size of a small railway carriage.

I said the area was much like Asakusa, but really it reminded me more of the scene at festivals in Tokyo's Kudanshita district, although it's been at least a decade since I attended one of those festivals.

Hanging around that district in Paris, I was surrounded, almost to the point where I couldn't walk, by types whose faces and manners were rougher than anything I'd ever encountered in Japan. It made me feel like I'd arrived in some savage land, not Europe.

Later, when I went to the upscale dance halls and cafés, far nicer than the ones in Asakusa, I was surprised to again encounter pool tables and roulette wheels.

In Lyon, I visited l'île Barbe—literally "Beard Island"—where people went to amuse themselves. It was a little islet in the north of the Saône, the river that runs through the heart of the city. But I saw few graybeards on that little island, which was as lively as the slums of Paris.

The square outside Lyon's main train station was also a lively place. At night you saw crowds of people, and again those billiard, roulette, and rifle games. And like Paris, there were streams of five- or ten-franc prostitutes. The pastimes of the French people seemed to be of this vulgar nature. [*Manuscript ends here.*]

A Note to My Comrades

First, let me sincerely ask forgiveness for disappearing so suddenly with only a word of explanation to a few close comrades at *Rōdō undō*, and for doing so at such a frenzied moment, just as our struggle for a federated labor union (instead of a centralized one) was getting started.

There is probably not much point in making this apology now, but things were too hectic to have made it earlier. And it was necessary to maintain almost complete secrecy about my trip. [*Manuscript ends here.*]

Ōsugi with his eldest daughter Mako (July 11, 1923).

Afterword to the 1923 ARS Edition

Our original plan was to publish *Nippon dasshutsu ki* around the middle of September. But the massive earthquake that struck Tokyo at the beginning of that month forced us to abandon the plan. And then, in the meantime, this book by our comrade Ōsugi became a posthumous work.

My last meeting with him was three days after the earthquake, at his house in Kashiwagi. As usual, he came down from the second floor to greet me wearing hardly anything.

"That earthquake came just in time," he said with a carefree laugh. "At least for a while no one will pester me to finish an article."

From the moment he returned from France, Ōsugi was busy working to finish this book and the autobiography that Kaizōsha planned to publish. An editor from ARS would stop by his house almost every day in those weeks before the earthquake to pressure him to finish the manuscript, returning to the office each time after prying away another ten or twenty pages. So for Ōsugi the earthquake brought some welcome relief from these intrusions.

He stayed with us at the office of *Rōdō undō* in Komagome for a little while after returning from France. But since he had so much work to do, and was so often being dragged to organizational meetings or hosting visitors, I didn't have the chance to hear more than a few snippets from him about his trip. This was also because I was away on my own trip for twenty days in August. By the time I returned, he had moved from the office to the house in Kashiwagi, leaving us with even fewer chances to meet. So reading this book has taught me many new things about his trip that I hadn't known, despite being one of his close comrades.

This afterword is not intended to present my recollections of Ōsugi, however. Rather, I want to explain a few things about the content of the book.

As I mentioned, the book originally was to be published in mid-September. Even before the earthquake, most of the book had been typeset by the printers. All that remained was for Ōsugi to finish the final chapter, "Assorted Stories from My Trip Overseas," and "A Note to My Comrades." In the end, though, neither was completed. After his death, we eventually came across the eighth and the incomplete ninth section of "Assorted Stories" and a fragment of "A Note" in his desk drawer.

Whether Ōsugi had intended to write much more for the

Afterword to the 1923 ARS Edition

final chapter, I don't know. Before the earthquake I recall that he said, "I could go on writing in this style for quite a while, but I'm not sure how it interesting it will be. Another two or three days would probably be enough." That leads me to believe that the final chapter contains more or less what he had intended to say.

"A Note" was something that we were going to publish in the monthly journal *Rōdō undō* and also use to conclude the book. But Ōsugi had only just started writing it and we are left with little idea of what he had planned to say. In any case, we have included the fragment of the note and the final nine pages of "Assorted Stories," which were both discovered after his death.

His article "The Anarchist General" (*Museifushugi shōgun*) is also included,* but it differs in nature from the other chapters. The article reflects the deep interest Ōsugi had in the Makhnovist movement near the end of his life. The extent of this interest is quite clear from the fact that he chose the name "Nestor" for his son who was born soon after Ōsugi's return from France. He said that his primary task while in France was to gather materials about the movement led by Nestor Makhno. It was terribly disappointing for Ōsugi that his inability to travel on to Germany robbed him of the chance to meet Voline,† who was known as Makhno's right-hand man.

---

* As noted in the Translator's Introduction, Ōsugi's article on Nestor Makhno, published in the ARS edition, was not included in subsequent editions of the book.

† Pseudonym of V. M. Eichenbaum, author of *The Unknown Revolution;*

My Escapes from Japan

The Makhnovist movement was one of the topics—along with the social situation in France—that my comrades and I most wanted to ask Ōsugi about. In this sense, it was natural for him to want to include the article in the book, despite its difference from the rest of the content.

The photograph[*] inserted at the beginning of the book was taken at the hotel in Kobe where Ōsugi stayed on the night of his return from France. It's the most recent photograph of him that I possess. I've included it because of the many passages in the book where Ōsugi recalls his daughter Mako, reflecting his great love for her and his general fondness for children.

Kondō Kenji[†]

Rōdō undō office, alongside the ashes of Ōsugi Sakae
October 16, 1923

1917–1921.

[*] The photograph on p.150.

[†] See footnote on p. 6.

Afterword to the English Edition

Nippon dasshutsu ki (My Escapes from Japan) is Ōsugi Sakae's final work. His autobiography was published just prior to it, but that book only covers the period up to around when Ōsugi, still a student at Foreign Language College in Tokyo, threw himself into the socialist movement, inspired by the opposition of Kōtoku Shūsui and others to the Russo-Japanese War. *Escapes* was meant to be the continuation of that autobiography—and it ended up being the final chapter, since just a month before its publication Ōsugi was murdered.

Eighteen years elapsed between Ōsugi's graduation from the college and his death in 1923. His aim during those years was to bring together the anarchists and syndicalists into a social movement aimed at transforming Japan. *Escapes* explains little of this political and social outlook, but it may be the best introduction to Ōsugi as a person, providing vivid accounts of the unbending yet open-minded way he carried out his activities.

In December 1922, Ōsugi "escaped" from Japan, where he had been under tight surveillance, to attend an international conference of anarchists that was to be held the following year in Berlin. But *Escapes* also documents how he slipped out of the country three years earlier to attend the Conference of Far-Eastern Socialists in Shanghai, revealing some of the inside story of that meeting.

Even though the Shanghai conference was organized by the Comintern, it took place around the time that the coalition-based Socialist League was formed in Japan. Ōsugi still held the hope then that anarchists and communists could work together, and that solidarity within an international movement was possible. Ōsugi always had a passion for close international ties, as reflected by the effort he made to teach Esperanto and classes on socialism to Chinese comrades living in Japan, and by his participation in the Asian Friendship Society made up of comrades of various nationalities hoping to forge an Asian federation.

After he returned to Japan from Shanghai in 1920, Ōsugi continued to pursue a united front between anarchists and communists. But his overtures were not reciprocated, and in *Escapes* he registers his pent-up frustration with the communists. The conflict came to a head in the *ana-bōru ronsō*, as it came to be known: the 1922 dispute between the anarchists and "Bolsheviks" (communists) that scuttled the effort to establish a trade-union coalition in Japan.

Afterword to the English Edition

Ōsugi's second "escape" from Japan took place at the height of that conflict between the anarchists and communists. He left the country to attend a planned conference in Berlin that was to create an international anarchist league. Ōsugi wanted to attend the conference to see for himself the postwar situation in European countries and also establish contact with comrades there. Another important aim for him was to better understand the revolutionary movement led by the Ukrainian anarchist Nestor Makhno that arose out of the Russian Revolution. Much of Ōsugi's time was spent researching the Makhnovist movement, although *Escapes* makes it seem that he had an easygoing stay in Paris.

Ultimately, the Berlin conference was postponed; Ōsugi never set foot in Germany; and on May 1, 1923, he was arrested in Paris for making a May Day speech. He spent almost a month in prison and was deported after his release.

Upon his return to Japan in early July, Ōsugi set about preparing a conference of anarchists. He wanted to drive the movement forward by forming an organization of anarchists or a free labor-union coalition. And so he attended labor-union meetings day and night and did his utmost rally his comrades.

In the midst of this activity, Tokyo was struck by the massive Great Kanto Earthquake on September 1. In the chaos that followed, Ōsugi was murdered along with his wife Itō Noe and six-year-old nephew Tachibana Munekazu at the hands of Amakasu Masahiko and other members of the military police. Half a century later an expert autopsy was discovered that revealed the violent assault that Ōsugi and Itō had

My Escapes from Japan

suffered: how their ribs had been smashed and the two had been kicked and trampled upon.

The murder took place on September 16. On that day, Ōsugi and Itō visited his younger brother's family, who had taken refuge from the disaster in Yokohama. They were returning to their own home along with their nephew when the three were waylaid by five members of Tokyo's military police and taken to police headquarters, where they were beaten to death.

The younger brother whom Ōsugi visited on that September day was my father, Isamu, and the house was my own birthplace. Since Ōsugi Sakae was the only blood relation my father was in close contact with, he certainly must have heard personal details about his older brother's life at the time and received some of the presents from Europe that are mentioned in *Escapes*. But I never had the chance to hear those stories from my father, who died when I was seven years old.

It was only many years later that I began to develop a deep interest in my uncle. Seeing my own children growing up, my feeling grew stronger that I should tell them something about the movement in which Ōsugi took part and about him as a person. And, as I mentioned, the work by him that seems to best convey his personality is *Escapes*. In it, he presents the sort of anecdotes about himself and the anarchist movement that I think he might have related personally to my father after returning from France.

The chapters that make up *Escapes* were first published as separate articles. "Escaping Japan" and "Prison Life until Deportation" were published in the July and September is-

Afterword to the English Edition

sues of the magazine *Kaizō*, respectively. "Toilets of Paris" and "Prison Songs" were each serialized in the newspaper *Tokyo nichinichi shimbun* (today's *Mainichi shimbun*), from June 22 to 24, and from July 13 to 14. At the time of his death, Ōsugi was still finishing up the chapter "Assorted Stories from My Trip Overseas" for the book. Sections of it were found in his desk, along with a few lines of a manuscript titled "A Note to My Comrades" that was to be published in the anarchist newspaper *Rōdō undō*.

Ōsugi Yutaka

In memory of my uncle, Ōsugi Sakae
October, 2014

MINISTÈRE DE L'INTÉRIEUR

RÉPUBLIQUE FRANÇAISE

**DIRECTION
de la Sûreté générale**

2ᵉ BUREAU

Police des Étrangers

EXPULSION

COPIE

LE MINISTRE DE L'INTÉRIEUR,

Vu l'article 7 de la loi des 13, 21 novembre, et 3 décembre 1849, ainsi conçu :

« Le Ministre de l'Intérieur pourra, par mesure de police, enjoindre à tout étranger voyageant ou résidant en France, de sortir immédiatement du territoire français et le faire conduire à la frontière. »

Vu l'article 8 de la même loi, ainsi conçu :

« Tout étranger qui se serait soustrait à l'exécution des mesures énoncées dans l'article précédent, ou qui, après être sorti de France par suite de ces mesures, y serait rentré sans permission du Gouvernement, sera traduit devant les tribunaux, et condamné à un emprisonnement d'un mois à six mois ;

» Après l'expiration de sa peine, il sera reconduit à la frontière. »

Considérant que la présence sur le territoire de la République, de l'étranger susdésigné est de nature à compromettre la sûreté publique;

Sur la proposition du

ARRÊTE :

Art. 1ᵉʳ.

Il est enjoint au nommé

de sortir du territoire français.

Art. 2.

Le Préfet de Police est chargé de l'exécution du présent arrêté.

Fait à Paris, le

Signé :

POUR AMPLIATION :
Pour le Directeur de la Sûreté Générale
LE CHEF DU 2ᵉ BUREAU
Signé

Signé :
Pour copie certifiée conforme
LE DIRECTEUR DU CABINET

Chronology of the "Escapes" (1920–23)[*]

1920

July	Attends meeting to prepare the formation of the Japan Socialist League.
Late Aug.	Visited by an envoy from the Korean provisional government in Shanghai, Yi Ch'un-suk. Accepts invitation to attend the Conference of Far-Eastern Socialists.
Early Oct.	Ivan Kozlov flees from creditors and hides out at Ōsugi's home in Kamakura before departing for Kobe.
Mid-Oct.	Chosen as an editorial board member of *Socialism*, the central organ of the Japan Socialist League.

---

[*] Based on the detailed chronology in Ōsugi Yutaka's 2009 book *Nichiroku: Ōsugi Sakae den* (A Record of the Life of Ōsugi Sakae).

Oct. 20	Sneaks out of his home with the help of Kuwabara Rentarō.
Oct. 25	Arrives in Shanghai in the midst of an anti-Japanese boycott. Meets with Chinese and Korean socialists and the Comintern representative.
Nov. 29	Returns to his home in Kamakura.
Dec. 10	Arrested along with 74 others at a meeting to announce formation of the Japan Socialist League.

1921

Jan. 25	First issue of the weekly *Rōdō undō* (The Labor Movement) published (dated Jan. 29).
Feb 15	Hospitalized for typhoid fever.
Mar. 13	Birth of his daughter Emma.
Mar. 28	Released from hospital.
Mid-Apr.	Meets the Comintern's secret envoy, Yi Ch'un-suk, and recommends that Kondō Eizō attend the 1922 Congress of the Toilers of the Far East in Moscow and Leningrad.
May 1	Japan's second May Day demonstrations held.
May 9	Arrested on way to attend the second congress of the Japan Socialist League.
May 28	Government orders the dissolution of the Japan Socialist League.
July 13	Commissioned by the publishing company Kaizōsha to write an autobiography.
July 26	Joins around 40 other Japanese intellectuals in attending a reception for Bertrand Russell organized by Kaizōsha.

Chronology of the "Escapes" (1920–23)

Early Oct.   Participates in meeting to choose delegates for the Congress of the Toilers of the Far East.

1922

June 7   Birth of his daughter Louise.
July 23   Deportation of Kozlov from Japan.
Sep. 30   Arrested at a meeting in Osaka to discuss formation of a trade-union confederation.
Oct. 14   Itō Noe travels to her hometown in Fukuoka Prefecture with her daughters Emma and Louise.
Nov. 20   Arrival of invitation from André Colomer to attend international anarchist conference.
Nov. 28 (?)   Visits the house of novelist Arishima Takeo to receive a 1,500-yen loan for the trip to Europe.
Late Nov.   Visits the printing shop of Yamaga Taiji to arrange for a fake Chinese passport.
Dec. 11   Sneaks out of his house to begin his trip to Europe; departs from Tokyo Station.
Dec. 12   Arrives in Kobe, where he spends two nights at a hotel.
Dec. 14   Sets sail from Kobe for Shanghai.
Dec 17 (?)   Arrives in Shanghai; stays at the Huaguang Hospital and at a nearby home of an English woman.
End of Dec.   Meets Yamaga Taiji, receives a Chinese passport secured with the help of comrades in Shanghai.

1923

Jan. 5   Boards the French ship André Lebon at Shanghai.

Jan. 28 (?)	Ship stops at Colombo, where Ōsugi goes ashore.
Feb. 13	Arrives in Marseille, spending the night there.
Feb. 14	Arrives in Lyon, where he spends a week with his Chinese comrades.
Feb 20 (?)	Travels to Paris, where he meets Colomer at the office of *le Libertaire*.
Feb. 21 (?)	Meets for several days with Chinese comrades on the outskirts of Paris.
Mar. 3	Visited by the painter Hayashi Shizue. The two move in to a hotel in Montmartre.
Mar. 18	Arrives in Lyon. Discusses matters with Chinese comrades.
Mar. 19	Travels to Marseille with Hayashi; they meet "Madame N." on the outskirts of the city.
Mar. 21	Returns to Lyon.
Mar. 28	Applies for permission at police headquarters to travel to Germany.
Apr. 9	Visited by Hayashi and the literary critic Komatsu Kiyoshi.
Apr. 22	Introduced by Hayashi to *Tokyo nichinichi shimbun* correspondent Izawa Hiroshi.
Apr. 26 (?)	Izawa visits Ōsugi again, accompanied by *Osaka mainichi shimbun* correspondent Kamoi.
Apr. 28	Travels to Paris.
Apr. 29	Visits Colomer; later meets Hayashi and the writer Satō Kōroku.
Apr. 30	Submits the article "Toilets of Paris" to Izawa. Has dinner near place de l'Opéra with a female friend.
May 1	Attends May Day meeting at a workers' hall in Saint

Chronology of the "Escapes" (1920–23)

	Denis; arrested after making a speech at the meeting.
May 2	Transferred to the Prefecture of Police in Paris, which investigates his case.
May 3	Detained at La Santé Prison.
May 16	Preliminary hearing of his case.
May 23	Receives a three-week prison sentence from the Paris court.
May 24	Released from prison, having already served his sentence during the investigation. Issued a deportation order by the police and sent to Marseille.
May 25	Arrives in Marseille. Visits the Japanese consulate to arrange return voyage to Japan. Stays at Hôtel Noyers for a week while awaiting departure.
May 31	Hayashi arrives in Marseille from Paris.
June 1	Visits Japanese consulate with Hayashi; receives second-class ticket to Japan. Later visits the nearby fishing village of l'Estaque.
June 2	Chinese comrades from Lyon visit Ōsugi. He buys gifts for friends and family back home.
June 3	Departs Marseille for Japan on the Nippon Yūsen ship Hakone Maru.
June 8	Ship stops in Port Said, where Ōsugi goes ashore.
June 29	Port of call in Colombo.
July 7	Arrives in Shanghai in the morning. Held in custody at the Japanese consulate. Boards the ship again the following day.
July 11	Arrives in Kobe. Meets his family and Yasutani Kan'ichi after undergoing an examination at the local police station.

July 12	Departs Kobe by train in the morning and arrives at Tokyo Station that evening. Returns to home in Komagome, Tokyo.
July 28	Attends a welcome home party with Itō Noe at Café Paulista in Ginza.
Aug. 9	Birth of his son Nestor.
Aug. 10	Completes manuscript for "Prison Life Until Deportation."
Sep. 1	Great Kantō Earthquake.
Sep. 16	Ōsugi and Itō Noe visit the Tsurumi section of Yokohama, where his younger brother Isamu had taken refuge with his family. Sets out with Itō and his nephew Munekazu to head home to Tokyo. The three are abducted by the Tokyo military police (*kempeitai*) and murdered the same day.
Oct. 25	ARS publishes *Nippon dasshutsu ki* (My Escapes from Japan).

ABOUT THE AUTHOR

ŌSUGI SAKAE was born in 1885, the son of a career military officer, and grew up in Niigata Prefecture. Moved to Tokyo in 1901 after expulsion from Nagoya Military Cadet School; enrolled the following year in Foreign Language College. In 1904, came into contact with the socialist movement through *Heimin shimbun* (Commoners' News), a radical, anti-war newspaper edited by Kōtoku Shūsui and Sakai Toshihiko. Married Hori Yasuko in 1906 and was arrested that year for taking part in a demonstration against a streetcar fare hike. Other arrests and prison sentences followed, including a sentence of two-and-a-half years for involvement in the 1908 Red Flag Incident. Released from prison in late 1910, around the time Kōtoku and other radicals were sentenced to death for their alleged involvement in a plot to assassinate the emperor. In 1912, helped to revive the chilled radical movement through establishing the literary journal *Kindai shisō* (Modern Thought) with Arahata Kanson. The journal was published until 1916. That same year his love affairs with Itō Noe and Kamichika Ichiko led to a public scandal that ended his marriage. Subsequently began living with Itō, with whom he established the journal *Bunmei hihyō* in 1918. Traveled to Shanghai in 1920 to attend the Comintern's Conference of Far-Eastern Socialists. Attempted to form a "united front" with communists in 1921 through the newspaper *Rōdō undō* (The Labor Movement), but soon parted ways with them. Departed Japan at the end of 1922 clandestinely to travel to Shanghai and then went on to Europe, where he hoped to attend an international anarchist conference. Arrested in France the following year for an incendiary speech delivered at a May Day meeting. Returned to Japan in July following his deportation from France. Abducted by the military police on September 16, 1923, and murdered along with Itō and his six-year-old nephew. A translator of numerous books, including Kropotkin's *Mutual Aid*, Darwin's *The Origin of Species*, and Fabre's *Souvenirs entomologiques*. His own works include *Sei no tōsō* (Struggle for Life; 1914), *Rōdō undo no tetsugaku* (Philosophy of the Labor Movement; 1916), *Kuropotokin kenkyū* (Studies of Kropotkin; 1920), and *Seigi o motomeru kokoro* (Justice-Seeking Spirit; 1921); and the memoirs *Gokuchūki* (Prison Memoirs; 1919) and *Jijoden* (Autobiography; 1923).

MICHAEL SCHAUERTE is a translator and writer. Has lived for the past twenty years in Japan. Graduated from Kenyon College in 1991 and received an MA from Hitotsubashi University in 2001. Writings on Ōsugi Sakae include "Shijin toshite no Ōsugi Sakae" (Ōsugi Sakae as Poet), published in the 2013 book *Ōsugi Sakae to nakamatachi* (Ōsugi Sakae and Friends). Regularly writes for the *Socialist Standard*. Now makes his home in Miyazaki Prefecture with his wife and two daughters.

ŌSUGI YUTAKA is the son of Ōsugi Sakae's younger brother, Isamu. A graduate of Tokyo Metropolitan University. Worked for the television broadcasting company TBS until his retirement in 1999. His detailed chronology of the life of Ōsugi Sakae, *Nichiroku: Ōsugi Sakae Den* (A Record of the Life of Ōsugi Sakae), was published in 2009. Currently a part-time instructor at Tōhō Gakuen and Tokiwa University.